I Didn't Know That
ALMANAC

CALIFORNIA EDITION

2007

COOL SPRINGS PRESS
A Division of Thomas Nelson Publishers
Since 1798

www.thomasnelson.com

Nashville, Tennessee

I DIDN'T KNOW THAT ALMANAC CALIFORNIA EDITION 2007

Copyright © 2006 by Cool Springs Press

Published by Cool Springs Press, a division of Thomas Nelson, Inc., P.O. Box 141000, Nashville, Tennessee, 37214.

First Printing 2006
Printed in the United States of America

Cover Design: Bruce Gore, Gore Studios
Writer: Jamie Chavez for WordWorks
Interior Design: Karen Williams [intudesign.net]

Cool Springs Press books may be purchased in bulk for educational, business, fundraising, or sales promotional use. For information, please e-mail **Special Markets@ThomasNelson.com.**

Visit the Cool Springs Web site at **www.CoolSpringsPress.net.**

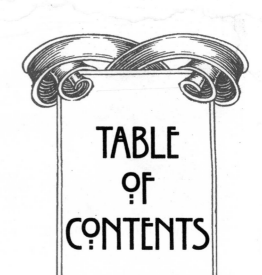

TABLE
OF
CONTENTS

CULTURE   5
& HISTORY

TRAVEL   34

WILDLIFE   58

BUSINESS   78

ENVIRONMENT   88

SPORTS   122

COOKING   141

GARDENING   169
& OUTDOORS

CALIFORNIA DREAMIN'

Hey, it doesn't have to be winter for us to daydream about the Golden State—because California is the stuff of which fantasies are surely made ... any time of year! From the young men who arrived during the Gold Rush to the Okies who looked for help here during the Depression, and every starry-eyed aspiring actress who leaves the Midwest for Hollywood today, the state has nurtured many a dream ... and made a few come true too.

A place that truly has to be seen and experienced to be appreciated, California is a state of extravagant contrasts: It's the produce basket of the nation ... and its playground too. It's the source of much of the world's entertainment ... and sometimes the butt of the world's jokes (and ask us if we care!). It's home to two of the nation's most iconic cities ... and hundreds of little hometowns that no one's ever heard of. From the Spanish to the Chinese to the Armenians and Laotians, California is a state that takes its strength from its diversity ... and celebrates it. Good vibrations? Oh yes, we've got 'em.

So have a look inside and discover all the things that are wonderful about the beautiful Golden State. We guarantee you'll be doing a little California dreamin' of your own!

What's in a Name?

The name California is thought to have emerged from a Spanish romance novel written in the early sixteenth century—some years before the Spanish "discovered" Baja California in 1533—about a mythical paradise called Califia. Written by García Ordóñez de Montalvo and called *The Exploits of the Very Powerful Cavalier Esplandián, Son of the Excellent King Amadis of Gaul,* the book describes an isolated island flowing with gold ruled over by a beautiful (but of course!) and free-spirited woman of Amazonian proportions whose name was Queen Califia.

Of course, the name California could just be derived from the Spanish for "hot as an oven"—*cali* deriving from *caliente* (hot) and *fornia* deriving from *fornalia* (oven, furnace).

We don't know about you, but we like the romance novel version!

Follow the
Mission Trail

Long inhabited by a diverse group of native peoples, the west coast of the American continent was visited sporadically by Europeans in the 1500s. Most of them thought the region was a large island for some two centuries, as maps from the period show.

It wasn't until 1769, when Spanish missionaries traveled up from Mexico, that a concerted effort was made to explore and settle the state. Led by Father Junipero Serra, twenty-one missions were established, starting in what is now San Diego and stretching up the coastline along El Camino Real (the King's Highway) to Sonoma, just north of the San Francisco Bay area.

It's said that Father Serra carried a pocketful of mustard seeds that he had brought from Spain, which he scattered to mark his trail. To this day, in early spring El Camino Real is ablaze with the yellow blooms of the mustard planted so long ago.

Mustard plant and seed.

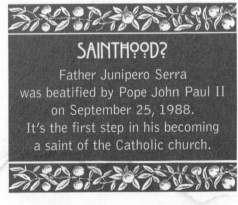

SAINTHOOD?

Father Junipero Serra was beatified by Pope John Paul II on September 25, 1988. It's the first step in his becoming a saint of the Catholic church.

CALIFORNIA POPPY

• The poppy may be one reason Califorinia is called the Golden State, but did you know that some folks think it's (gasp!) a weed? Recognized as a "potentially invasive" species, the California poppy is classified as a Rank 3 (Lesser Threat) in Tennessee and other states.

• April 6th each year is California Poppy Day.

• Contrary to popular belief, it is not illegal to pick the poppies because it is the state flower! (However, it is a misdemeanor to cut or remove any flower, tree, shrub, or other plant growing along state highways or in state parks.)

• Look for poppies in the Antelope Valley California Poppy Preserve in northern Los Angeles County; the peak spring display (timing is unpredictable, although early April is likely) is incredible.

• The poppy grows best in "disturbed" areas; disturbances can be man-made (construction or farming) or natural (fires or animal trails and grazing).

The California Poppy Festival

Every April, the city of Lancaster hosts its annual poppy festival, featuring arts and crafts, a flower and farmers market, aerospace and aviation displays, headline musical acts, and lots of local wildflowers. Pick up a free wildflower maps and learn about the best viewing locations before heading out to the Antelope Valley California Poppy Reserve.

LANCASTER CITY PARK, 43011 N. 10TH ST. W., LANCASTER 93534 / (661) 723-6077.

NAPA VALLEY MUSTARD FESTIVAL

A SENSATIONAL SEASON OF WINE COUNTRY EVENTS!

Every February and March, visit the Napa Valley when the mustard's in bloom, and enjoy great food, wine, art, and cultural and entertainment activities.

Napa Valley Mustard Festival
P.O. Box 3603
Yountville, CA 94599
(707) 944-113

Hush! It's a Gold Rush!

Pity poor John Sutter (1803–1880). Broke as a result of a failed business venture in his homeland, Switzerland, he traveled to California for a fresh start in 1839. He called his settlement New Helvetia (New Switzerland), and proceeded to establish a fort that, for a time, was the end point for all new arrivals in California territory, mostly due to his reputation for kindness and hospitality.

John Augustus Sutter

Later, Sutter built a lumber mill on the American River, fifty-four miles up into the foothills from New Helvetia, and had plans to establish an agricultural empire ... which is why—when his employee James Marshall announced he'd discovered a gold chip in the river on January 24, 1848—Sutter would have preferred that the news be kept quiet.

But by mid-August of that year, the New York newspapers were reporting the find, and before long the rush was on. Sutter's farmhands deserted and his property was overrun with prospectors, virtually ruining him a second time.

WHAT'S AN ARGONAUT?

"Forty-Niner" is the name given to the roughly 70,000 young men who left cities and farms across the United States and traveled west to California in 1849 ... the men who created the California Gold Rush. Two years later, the population of San Francisco alone had increased by some 86,000! The miners called themselves the Argonauts—after the mythical Jason and his golden fleece.

I DIDN'T KNOW THAT ALMANAC CALIFORNIA EDITION 2007

THE MAN WHO TRIGGERED A GOLD RUSH

Sam Brannan (1819–1889), a printer, planned on building an empire in California when he arrived at what is now San Francisco in 1846. He founded the city's first newspaper, the *California Star*, and shortly thereafter moved to John Sutter's settlement and opened a general store. When someone paid in gold for goods in Brannan's store, he drew his own conclusions, but when a March 25 article in the *Star* did not raise any excitement, Brannan himself traveled to San Francisco, stood on a street corner with a bottle of gold dust, and shouted "Gold! Gold! Gold from the American River!" Well, *that* did it.

A California stagecoach schedule to bring in prospective miners.

TALK ABOUT THE HIGH COST OF LIVING!

As you'd expect, the California Gold Rush created inflation in prices of just about everything. During a time when laborers in the East earned less than a dollar a day, costs in California were skyrocketing…

Overland journey in wagon train: $200

Sugar, 2 cups: $1.50

Flour, 2 cups: $1.00

Coffee, 2 cups: $1.00

Liquor, 2 cups: $4.00

Bowl of bean soup: $1.00

Serving of roast beef: $1.50

Serving of bacon: $1.00

Rice pudding with molasses: $1.00

A California gold rush town.

NORTH

BERKELEY ART MUSEUM & PACIFIC FILM ARCHIVE
(510) 642-0808
2626 Bancroft Way, Berkeley, CA 94720
Founded by UC-Berkeley art teacher, with strengths in Asian and California art.

CALIFORNIA ACADEMY OF SCIENCES
(415) 321-8000
875 Howard St., San Francisco, CA 94103-3098
Explore earth, sea, and space.

CALIFORNIA STATE RAILROAD MUSEUM
(916) 447-4363
111 "I" St., Sacramento, CA 95814
Once the terminus of the Transcontinental Railway.

CROCKER ART MUSEUM
(916) 264-5423
216 "O" St., Sacramento, CA 95814
Founded by California pioneer family.

EXPLORATORIUM
(415) 397-5673
3601 Lyon St., San Francisco, CA 94123
Fun science museum of technology, nature, and art.

THE NATIONAL STEINBECK CENTER
(831) 796-3833
One Main St., Salinas, CA 93901
A journey through John Steinbeck's world.

OAKLAND MUSEUM OF CALIFORNIA
(510) 238-2200
1000 Oak St., Oakland, CA 94607
Devoted to the art, history, and natural sciences of California.

PALACE OF THE LEGION OF HONOR
100 34th Ave., San Francisco, CA 94122
(415) 750-3600
European art in a neoclassic beaux-arts building.

SAN FRANCISCO MUSEUM OF MODERN ART
(415) 357-4000
151 Third St., San Francisco, CA 94103-3107
Even the landmark building is a work of art.

SAN JOSE MUSEUM OF ART
(408) 271-6840
110 S. Market St., San Jose, CA 95113
Free admission!

SOUTH

AUTRY NATIONAL CENTER
(323) 667-2000
4700 Western Heritage Way, Los Angeles, CA 90027
Intercultural history in three important museums: cowboys, Indians, and women!

J. PAUL GETTY MUSEUM AT THE GETTY CENTER
(310) 440-7330
1200 Getty Center Dr., Los Angeles, CA 90049
Panoramic city and ocean views; free admission.

HUNTINGTON LIBRARY, ART GALLERIES AND BOTANICAL GARDENS
(626) 405-2100
1151 Oxford Rd., San Marino, CA 91108
Gainsborough's "Blue Boy" just one in this world-class museum and botanical gardens.

LOS ANGELES COUNTY MUSEUM OF ART
(323) 857-6000
5905 Wilshire Blvd., Los Angeles, CA 90036
A world-class permanent collection.

MUSEUM OF CONTEMPORARY ART
(213) 621-2766
250 S. Grand Ave., Los Angeles, CA 90012
Works created since 1940.

MUSEUMS OF BALBOA PARK
(619) 239-0512
1549 El Prado, Ste. #1, San Diego, CA 92101
Too many to list; days of interesting viewing.

MUSEUM OF TOLERANCE
(310) 553-8403
9786 W. Pico Blvd., Los Angeles, CA 90035
Highly recommended.

NORTON SIMON MUSEUM
(626) 449-6840
411 W. Colorado Blvd., Pasadena, CA 91105
Two thousand years of art redesigned by Frank O. Gehry.

PETERSEN AUTOMOTIVE MUSEUM
(323) 964-6331
6060 Wilshire Blvd., Los Angeles, CA 90036
Life-size period dioramas starring, yes, cars.

SANTA BARBARA MUSEUM OF ART
(805) 963-4364
1130 State St., Santa Barbara, CA 93101-2746
Unique character specific to this area.

CUE THEME FROM TWILIGHT ZONE

OK, we're gonna say it: this place is just weird. Or funny. Or wonderful ... depending on your point of view. In any case, it will be one of your most memorable museum experiences ever. A cross between a natural history museum and a museum of, well, oddities, the Museum of Jurassic Technology (don't ask, we don't know!) offers everything from low-tech dioramas to high tech-interactive displays that explore neglected or eccentric areas of natural science.

The Museum of Jurassic Technology
9341 Venice Boulevard
Culver City 90232 / (310) 836-6131

You'll Leave Smiling

The Burlingame Museum of Pez Memorabilia says it's just five minutes south of SFO, and we're not sure just how many folks disembark and head straight there ... but they should! After all, it's the only place in the world to see every single Pez dispenser ever made—over 550 at the moment. You'll see everything from Disney's Thumper to Darth Vader, including the rarest Pez—a Mr. Potato Head from 1973, taken off the market due to the choking hazard presented by the tiny pieces.

214 California Dr., Burlingame 94010 / (650) 347-2301

DID YOU KNOW?

• Pez hit the market in 1927, although the first containers were tin and did not have heads.
• The original Pez candies were peppermint—in fact, the name comes from the German word for peppermint (**pfefferminz**).
• The first Pez dispensers (not just a tin box) appeared around 1950.
• The first Pez dispensers with lifting cartoon heads appeared in 1952 (it was Mickey Mouse).
• When Pez added heads, the candy changed from peppermint to fruit flavors, as they are today.
• The Elvis Pez that appeared in the movie **The Client** was a prototype, never a production model.

It's All Politics!

The raging politics leading up to the Civil War influenced everything else going on around the continent—including statehood for California. The territory had been ceded to the U.S. at the end of the Mexican-American War, in the Treaty of Guadalupe-Hidalgo, signed on February 2, 1848. *But what in the world were they supposed to do with it?* The bitter debates in Congress had to do with whether or not slavery would be permitted here. In what has become known as the Compromise of 1850, it was decided that California would be admitted as a free state (Texas had just been annexed as a slaveholding state), *if* the territories of Utah and New Mexico were organized with no reference to slavery at all. At last, on August 13, 1850, the act admitting California as the thirty-first state of the union passed the Senate; it passed the House on September 7, and two days later, President Millard Fillmore signed it into law.

DID YOU KNOW?

The oldest fossil from the La Brea Tar Pit is a wood fragment dated at around 40, 000 years old (using the Carbon-14 method).

Tar Baby!

The Spanish missionaries were the first white men to see what we now call the La Brea Tar Pits. Father Crespi noted in his journal that they "saw some large marshes of a certain substance like pitch; they were boiling and bubbling, and the pitch came out mixed with an abundance of water."

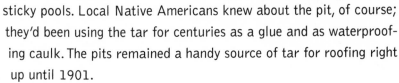

It was oil they saw, crude oil seeping to the surface and collecting in sticky pools. Local Native Americans knew about the pit, of course; they'd been using the tar for centuries as a glue and as waterproofing caulk. The pits remained a handy source of tar for roofing right up until 1901.

That was when that the first scientific excavation of the pits occurred. You see, there'd always been bones in the pits, and everyone just assumed they were the remains of unlucky cattle. But in 1901 a research team from UC–Berkeley were startled to learn that the La Brea Tar Pits contained thousands of Ice Age fossils— Pleistocene vertebrates, including at least 59 species of mammal and over 135 species of birds, as well as plants, mollusks, and insects, dating from 40,000 to 8,000 years ago!

Today there's a museum next door to the pit that displays many of the fossils and tells their story. The bones are brown from having lain in the asphalt all these years.

PAGE MUSEUM AT THE LA BREA TAR PITS
5801 WILSHIRE BLVD., LOS ANGELES 90036
(323) 934-7243

THE STATE FOSSIL

Wolves are the most common mammal found in the La Brea Tar Pit, but the second most common is *Smilodon californicus*—you know it as the sabre-toothed cat. Today it is the California state fossil, having been so designated in January, 1974.

TAKE ME TO YOUR LEADER

OR AT LEAST YOUR GOVERNOR

Peter Hardeman Burnett / 1849–1851

John McDougall / 1851–1852

John Bigler / 1852–1856

John Neeley Johnson / 1856–1858

John B. Weller / 1858–1860

Milton Slocum Latham / 1860–1860

John Gately Downey / 1860–1862

Amasa Leland Stanford / 1862–1863

Frederick Ferdinand Low / 1863–1867

Henry Huntly Haight / 1867–1871

Newton Booth / 1871–1875

Romualdo Pacheco (acting) / 1875–1875

William Irwin / 1875–1880

George Clement Perkins / 1880–1883

George Stoneman / 1883–1887

Washington Montgomery Bartlett / 1887–1887

Robert Whitney Waterman / 1887–1891

Henry Harrison Markham / 1891–1895

James Herbert Budd / 1895–1899

Henry Tifft Gage / 1899–1903

George Cooper Pardee / 1903–1907

James Norris Gillett / 1907–1911

Hiram Warren Johnson / 1911–1917

William Dennison Stephens / 1917–1923

Friend William Richardson / 1923–1927

Clement Calhoun Young / 1927–1931

James Rolph Jr. / 1931–1934

Frank Finley Merriam / 1934–1939

Culbert Levy Olson / 1939–1943

Earl Warren / 1943–1953

Goodwin Jess Knight / 1953–1959

Edmund Gerald "Pat" Brown Sr. / 1959–1967

Ronald Wilson Reagan / 1967–1975

Edmund Gerald "Jerry" Brown Jr. / 1975–1983

George Deukmejian / 1983–1991

Peter Barton Wilson / 1991–1999

Graham "Gray" Davis Jr. / 1999–2003

Arnold Alois Schwarzenegger / 2003–

Governor George Stoneman was a Union Clavary General during the Civil War.

Governor Ronald Reagan went on to become the 40th president of the United States.

FROM THE GIPPER TO THE GOVERNATOR
... CELEBRITIES AS POLITICIANS

1) Sonny Bono, singer (U.S. Representative, California)

2) Shirley Temple Black, child actress (U.S. diplomat)

3) Clint Eastwood, actor/director (mayor of Carmel, California)

4) Helen Gahagan, actress (U.S. Representative, California)

5) George Murphy, dancer/actor (U.S. Senator, California)

6) Ronald Reagan, actor (governor of California, U.S. president)

7) Arnold Schwarzenegger, actor (governor of California)

8) Sheila Kuehl, child actress (California state senator)

"Ronnie" ...

- Had several nicknames including Ronnie, Dutch, the Gipper, the Teflon President, the Great Communicator
- Born in Tampico, Illinois, February 6, 1911
- The 33rd governor of California and the 40th president of the U.S.
- First presidential role was of the Screen Actors Guild (1947–1952)
- Final movie role was in the 1964 film **The Killers**
- The oldest person ever elected president (age 69)
- The only divorced president
- His administration was followed by another Republican president—for the first time in 60 years
- The only U.S. president to be shot and survive an assassination attempt while in office
- Started his career as a radio announcer for Chicago Cubs baseball games
- The only U.S. president to have a star on Hollywood's Walk of Fame

"The latest polls show that Arnold Schwarzenegger is trailing Lieutenant Governor Cruz Bustamante in the polls. That's insane. I mean, think about it, this guy Cruz Bustamante has never even been in a movie."

—DAVID LETTERMAN, 2003

The Oldest Professional Ballet Company in America

The San Francisco Ballet has built a world-class reputation based on its many ballet "firsts" that give it a strong classical background, as well as its wonderful contemporary repertoire. Founded as the San Francisco Opera Ballet in 1933 (it became separate from the Opera in 1942), it is one of the three largest ballet companies in the United States.

- First American production of *Coppélia*
- First complete production of *Swan Lake* in the U.S.
- First complete production of *The Nutcracker* in the U.S.
- First to launch *The Nutcracker* as a Christmas Eve tradition (1944)
- First American ballet company to tour the Far East (1957)
- First televised performance of *The Nutcracker* (ABC, 1964)
- The Ballet also has its own academy, the San Francisco Ballet School

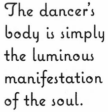

The dancer's body is simply the luminous manifestation of the soul.
—ISADORA DUNCAN
(1877–1927)

Known as the Mother of Modern Dance, Isadora Duncan was born in San Francisco, the child of parents who had come to California during the Gold Rush.

ALLENSWORTH:
THE TOWN THAT REFUSED TO DIE

Although the Emancipation Proclamation and the end of the Civil War had freed thousands of African-Americans from bondage, racism and existing laws throughout the country still effectively prevented African-Americans from fully pursuing the American Dream—until Union Army veteran Lieutenant Colonel Allen Allensworth founded a town near Bakersfield in 1909.

The donated land, around a train depot called Solito, became the first and only California town to be all–African-American founded, financed, and governed. The town thrived until around 1915 (and had residents until the late 1960s), but a variety of factors, from to controversy over its water supply to problems with the railroad to racism (the railroad, for example, refused to hire African-Americans), contributed to its decline, although it was the death of its founder that really took the heart out of Allensworth.

Today the deserted town is coming back to life as a California State Historic Park, with continuing restoration, special events, and an annual rededication ceremony. You can find it 20 miles north of Wasco on Highway 43; seven miles west of Earlimart on County Road J22.

There is much latent force both in men and women of which the world knows nothing, simply because the conditions of their lives are such that their strongest gifts remain dormant.

—COLONEL ALLEN ALLENSWORTH

Grapes of Wrath

CESAR CHAVEZ AND THE UNITED FARM WORKERS

Those who grew up in the '60s and '70s remember the grapes. And the lettuce. Cesar Chavez and the National Farm Workers Association (NFWA)—which he'd cofounded in 1962 with Dolores Huerta—led the now-historic strike of California grape-pickers in 1965, in protest of extremely low wages; he urged us to boycott table grapes to draw attention to the plight of migrant farm workers. The strike lasted five long years, but it worked, and the union evolved into the United Farm Workers (UFW), the first-ever union for farm workers. Chavez's career as a labor leader was ignited.

Born in Yuma, Arizona, Chavez's poorly educated Spanish-speaking parents lost their farm and country store during the Depression to unscrupulous businessmen, and moved the family of five children to California, where they embarked on the life of the migrant worker. By the time he dropped out after eighth grade, Cesar Chavez had attended 37 schools. Education would later become his passion; he was a lifelong reader.

Committed to the dignity of farm workers, Chavez utilized nonviolent tactics such as boycotts, pickets, strikes, and fasts to draw attention to *La Causa* (the cause). Although he never earned more than $5000 a year, Chavez was rich in respect and admiration. A year after his death, he was awarded the Medal of Freedom, America's highest civilian honor.

> Most farm workers in California make the minimum wage of $6.75 an hour. Virtually no workers have health insurance or paid vacations, although most are out of work for two or more months each year due to the cyclical nature of the crops.

Nonviolence really rests on the reservoir that you have to create in yourself of patience, not of being patient with the problems, but being patient with yourself to do the hard work.

—CESAR CHAVEZ

GOLD MOUNtAiN

Although we see folks of Chinese descent everywhere in California—in the arts, in politics, in academia, in business—and their contribution to the state cannot be underestimated, barely 150 years ago the Chinese had just arrived. Leaving poverty and constant war conditions behind, more than 2.5 million Chinese left their homeland before 1900.

- The first Chinese immigrants (two men and one woman) arrived in San Francisco in 1848
- San Francisco became known as Gum Saan ("Gold Mountain")— a wonderful place of freedom and prosperity
- Immigrants coming to the California Gold Rush were called "Gold Mountain Travelers"
- More than 322,000 Chinese came to the United States between 1850 and 1882

Sadly, the Chinese quickly encountered racial discrimination in their new country—even though their labor was needed to build railroads, work farms, and provide services.

- By 1859, Chinese children were not permitted into any public schools in San Francisco except the "Chinese School"
- In 1862, the Anti-Coolie Tax was passed—to discourage Chinese immigration to California
- Queues (the long tail of hair customarily worn by men) were banned in 1870, along with other anti-Chinese ordinances
- The Chinese Exclusion Act banned Chinese immigration altogether, and prohibited the Chinese already in the U.S. from becoming naturalized citizens

In 1934, Hollywood began enforcing California's antimiscegenation laws, preventing Chinese actors from playing romantic roles opposite non-Asian actors!

The Chinese Exclusion Act was not repealed until 1943, and antimiscegenation laws existed in California until 1948.

MIGRANT WORKERS' FRIEND

At age twenty-three, Dorothea Lange moved to San Francisco, where she opened a portrait photography studio at 540 Sutter Street. And there she might have stayed, making beautiful pictures of wealthy society matrons and their children. She did live in the city by the Bay for the rest of her life (another forty-seven years)—but it was her photographs of the poor and rootless migrant workers in California that made her famous. Compelled by the Great Depression (suddenly portrait photographs were economically irrelevant), Lange was employed by California's State Emergency Relief Administration to document working conditions for agricultural workers. Lange's work on this project (and that of Paul Schuster Taylor, later her husband) led directly to the establishment of the first government-funded public housing in the state in 1935. Late in life, she was the sixth photographer—and first woman—to be invited to have a one-person exhibition at New York's Museum of Modern Art.

This photograph, known as "Migrant Mother," is probably Lange's most famous. It depicts destitute pea pickers in California, centering on a mother of seven children, age thirty-two, in Nipomo, California, March 1936. The woman in the picture is Florence Owens Thompson, whose husband and sons had gone to get help for their broken down car.

While there is perhaps a province in which the photograph can tell us nothing more than what we see with our own eyes, there is another in which it proves to us how little our eyes permit us to see.

—DOROTHEA LANGE
(1896–1965)

CALIFORNIA POPULATION BY ETHNICITY
Source: U.S. Census Bureau, 2000

33,871,648	Total Population
20,170,059	White
5,682,241	Some other (single) race*
3,697,513	Asian
2,263,882	African-American or Black
1,607,646	Two or more races
333,346	American Indian and Alaska Native
116,961	Native Hawaiian and Other Pacific Islander

* mostly Hispanic or Latino, although some 10,966,556 claim to be Hispanic or Latino either as a single race or in combination with others listed above.

CALIFORNIA STATE SYMBOLS

Animal: California Grizzly Bear (*Ursus californicus*)

Bird: California Valley Quail (*Lophortyx californica*)

Fish: California Golden Trout (*Salmo agua-bonita*)

Flower: Golden Poppy (*Eschsholzia*)

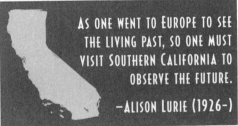

The state flag of California.

Insect: California Dogface Butterfly (*Zerene eurydice*)

Marine Fish: Garibaldi (*Hypsypops rubicundus*)

Marine Mammal: California Gray Whale (*Eschrichtius robustus*)

Reptile: Desert Tortoise (*Gopherus agasizzi*)

Tree: California Redwood (Coast Redwood: *Sequoia sempervirens*)

AS ONE WENT TO EUROPE TO SEE THE LIVING PAST, SO ONE MUST VISIT SOUTHERN CALIFORNIA TO OBSERVE THE FUTURE.

—ALISON LURIE (1926–)

In 1925 a giant sequoia located in Kings Canyon National Park was named the nation's national Christmas tree. The tree is over 300 feet tall.

The Real McCoy

Visitors to historic railroad town of Truckee are usually charmed by its old-fashioned look and nostalgic feel ... personified in the Truckee Diner. Originally prefabricated buildings, diners of a century ago were put on wheels and sent by rail or truck to their destinations—and this 1948

Kullman Dining Car Company original is just such a restaurant. However, this diner actually spent most of its life as the Birmingham Grille—in Philadelphia, Pennsylvania! Current owners bought the movable restaurant and had it trucked to California in 1995, where it was first lovingly restored and then opened for busi-ness...serving up good old-time comfort food to locals and tourists.

It took two months to move the Truckee Diner across the country. Be sure to step into the back hall and read the newspaper clippings that detail the adventure!

THE GOLDEN STATE'S 15 LARGEST CITIES

RANK	CITY	POPULATION	COUNTY
1.	Los Angeles	3,957,875	Los Angeles
2.	San Diego	1,305,736	San Diego
3.	San Jose	944,857	Santa Clara
4.	San Francisco	799,263	San Francisco
5.	Long Beach	491,564	Los Angeles
6.	Fresno	464,727	Fresno
7.	Sacramento	452,959	Sacramento
8.	Oakland	412,318	Alameda
9.	Santa Ana	351,697	Orange
10.	Anaheim	345,317	Orange
11.	Bakersfield	307,471	Kern
12.	Riverside	285,537	Riverside
13.	Stockton	279,800	San Joaquin
14.	Chula Vista	217,543	San Diego
15.	Fremont	210,445	Alameda

DO YOU KNOW THE WAY
TO SAN JOSE...OR TOADTOWN?

5 Brooks	Fort Dick	Rancho Cucamonga
Antlers	Freedom	Roads End
Aromas	Fruitland	Rough and Ready
Asylum	Frying Pan	Scarface
Avocado	Gas Point	Secret Town
Badwater	Hallelujah Junction	Siberia
Bagdad	Hardy	Skidoo
Bee Rock	Harmony	Sky High
Bivalve	Hellhole Palms	Soapweed
Blunt	Hells Kitchen	Soda Springs
Bumblebee	Honda	Squabbletown
Bummerville	Honeydew	Stovepipe
Burnt Ranch	Hooker	Sucker Flat
Cabbage Patch	Igo	Surf
Cactus	Jupiter	Surfside
Chiquita	Keg	Surprise
Clapper Gap	King Salmon	Tarzana
Confidence	Last Chance	Teakettle Junction
Cool	Little Penny	Timbuctoo
Cow Creek	Mad River	Toadtown
Dairyville	Mormon Bar	Truths Home
Date City	Mystic	Twentynine Palms
Deadman Crossing	Needles	Volcano
Deadwood	Nervo	Weed
Doghouse Junction	Ono	Weedpatch
Dogtown	Orange	Whiskeytown
Dunmovin	Peanut	Wimp
Eureka	Pixley	Woody
Fair Play	Plaster City	You Bet
Fallen Leaf	Prunedale	
False Klamath	Pumpkin Center	
Forks of Salmon	Ragtown	

THE BEAUTIFUL GOLDEN GATE

THEY TALKED ABOUT IT for years before they did it. Build the bridge, that is. Obviously it was a good idea to link the city of San Francisco with Marin County to the north. Ultimately, it took the passion of Joseph Strauss, an engineer who'd built over 400 bridges, to make a convincing case (he started presenting plans for the bridge in 1921), and construction began on January 5, 1933, with Strauss as chief engineer. Irving Morrow, the consulting architect, added Art Deco touches to the design, and was responsible for the choice of color, while Leon Moisseiff, a bridge designer, offered help with the complicated mathematics involved in the plans.

The bridge was opened to vehicular traffic on May 28, 1937, and has only been closed three times since then, all for high winds (well, OK, it was closed twice, very briefly, for visiting dignitaries—President Franklin D. Roosevelt and French president Charles de Gaulle—and is sometimes closed in the middle of the night, albeit briefly, for construction activities). The 1989 Loma Prieta earthquake didn't even faze it.

Yes, But Orange?

Irving Morrow was responsible for choosing "International Orange" for the bridge. He rejected both black and gray and chose instead a color that would be easily visible in the frequent San Francisco fog (if the U.S. Navy had its way, the bridge would be striped black and yellow!) and yet would have aesthetic appeal in its natural setting. The American Society of Civil Engineers designated the bridge one of the Seven Wonders of the Modern World.

World's Leading Suicide Location

- On the average, the Golden Gate Bridge has a jumper every two weeks.

- At least 1200 people have been seen jumping or were found in the water since the bridge opened (they quit counting in 1995). This doesn't count those who may have jumped at night or were never found.

- The fall takes 4 seconds; jumpers hit the water going 75 mph.

- As of 2006, only 26 people have survived the jump.

- There is a suicide hotline phone located on the bridge.

Did You Know...?

- The Golden Gate Bridge has only been painted from end-to-end twice. But it has a full-time crew of 38 painters who handle touch-up painting on an on-going basis.

- The bridge is named after the Golden Gate Strait, the narrow, 3-mile strait that leads from the Pacific Ocean to San Francisco Bay.

- The Golden Gate had the longest suspension span (the distance between the towers) in the world from the time of its construction until 1964, when the Verrazano Narrows Bridge was completed in New York City. Today it is the seventh longest suspension bridge in the world.

- Eleven men lost their lives building the bridge.

- 1,779,032,891 vehicles had crossed the bridge as of June 2005 (which includes both northbound and southbound traffic).

GREAT CALIFORNIA ARCHITECTURE

Grandfather of the California Ranch-Style

The architectural predecessor to the ubiquitous ranch-style home that so many of us live in today is a style called Craftsman. You can see Craftsman homes all over California if you know what you're looking for:

- street-facing gables
- low-pitched rooflines, usually shingled
- wide overhanging eaves, with exposed rafters underneath
- deep front porch underneath extension of the main roof
- square columns
- dark wood paneling
- arched opening separating the living and dining rooms
- large fireplace, often stone
- mixed materials throughout, usually local

The Craftsman style—which encompassed bungalows popularized by the architect brothers Charles and Henry Greene as well as the Prairie School of Frank Lloyd Wright and the mission oak style from designer Gustav Stickley—grew out of the Arts & Crafts Movement. It was primarily a reaction against the Industrial Revolution and the architecture it reflected moved away from the fussiness of Victorian homes while emphasizing natural materials.

California Craftsman Buildings
- Chick House (1913) / Bernard Maybeck
  7133 Chabot Rd., Oakland
- First Church of Christ Scientist (1910) / Bernard Maybeck
  2619 Dwight Way, Berkeley
- Gamble House (1909) / Green and Greene
  4 Westmoreland Place, Pasadena
- D. L. James House (1918) / Greene and Greene
  Hwy. 1, Carmel Highlands
  - Marston House (1905) / Hebbard and Gill
    3525 Seventh Ave., Balboa Park, San Diego

DESIGN BY EAMES

You've seen the ubiquitous Eames chair, but did you know that Charles and Ray Eames (Ray was his wife, a Californian) started as architects? Or that they maintained an office at 901 Washington Boulevard in Venice for forty-five years? Charles studied architecture briefly at St. Louis's prestigious Washington University in the mid-1920s but was dismissed because his "views were too modern"—so instead he just opened his own architecture firm! Later picking up his studies, he began to design award-winning furniture, and, during World War II, splints and stretchers for the U.S. Navy. Many of the Eames designs are still produced today. By this time the Eameses had moved to the Los Angeles area, where Charles continued to design modern homes with striking simplicity into the 1960s (after which he concentrated on furniture design, filmmaking, and exhibition design).

Today you can see the house Charles and Ray designed for themselves; it houses the Eames Office, which is dedicated to communicating and preserving the work of Charles and Ray. It is not open to the public, but you can schedule an appointment to view the outside of the building by calling (310) 459-9663. The house is located at 203/205 Chautauqua Blvd., in Santa Monica.

Ray Eames died in Los Angeles in 1988, ten years to the day after Charles (August 21).

> If Craftsman is the grandfather, then Prairie School homes are the father of modern California ranch homes. These homes are characterized by a long, low, horizontal shape; low-pitched roof; high windows or indirect lighting; and simplicity. For an example, see the Stewart House (1909) at Summit and Hot Springs roads, in Monteceito.

California Dreamin'

You won't find this as a section in your local bookstore, but California has been richly served in literature, by native Californians and others who were just observing. From Mark Twain's wonderful short story "The Celebrated Jumping Frog of Calaveras County" to John Steinbeck's social commentary in *The Grapes of Wrath*, to Raymond Chandler's moody *The Big Sleep*, your local library is full of books that evoke California as a place, as a metaphor, or even a state of mind. We recommend:

- Gertrude Atherton / *The Californians*
- James M. Cain / *Mildred Pierce*
- Joan Didion / *Run River*
- John Fante / *Ask the Dust*
- Jack Kerouac / *Big Sur*
- Jack London / *Sea Wolf*
- William Saroyan / *The Human Comedy*
- John Steinbeck / *Tortilla Flat*
- Robert Louis Stevenson / *The Silverado Squatters*
- Nathaniel West / *The Day of the Locust*

Charles Bukowski's gravestone reads: "Don't Try."

We Don't Care How They Do It In New York!

These Californians are all Pulitzer Prize winners:

Herb Caen [journalism]
Sidney Howard [drama]
Carolyn Kizer [poetry]
George Oppen [poetry]
William Saroyan [fiction]
Upton Sinclair [fiction, non-fiction]
Gary Snyder [poetry]
Wallace Stegner [fiction, non-fiction]
John Steinbeck [fiction]
Allan Temko [belles lettres]
Alice Walker [fiction, poetry]

*Nobel Prize for Literature
Czeslaw Milosz [poetry, belles lettres]
John Steinbeck [fiction]

Mom Always Liked You Best!

There was bound to be a bit of "sibling rivalry" in a state this big! After all, Southern California—SoCal in the vernacular—gets an awful lot of attention. It's the second-most populated area in the nation (after the Boston-NYC-Baltimore-Philadelphia-DC megalopolis) and, well, it does have all those movie stars. How far north does SoCal go? We're callin' the border at the Tehachapi Mountains, about 70 miles north of Los Angeles.

So does that mean everything north of Bakersfield is, *ipso facto*, Northern California (or NorCal as the locals say)? Um, no. At best, NorCal is the northern half of the state. Oh, it's beautiful all right. San Francisco, the sequoias...but let's not forget the San Joaquin Valley, playing the middle child to the South and the North.

CALIFORNIA

Totaling nearly three million acres, San Bernardino County is the largest county in the country.

CALIFORNIA COUNTIES			
Alameda	Kings	Placer	Shasta
Alpine	Lake	Plumas	Sierra
Amador	Lassen	Riverside	Siskiyou
Butte	Los Angeles	Sacramento	Solano
Calaveras	Madera	San Benito	Sonoma
Colusa	Marin	San Bernardino	Stanislaus
Contra Costa	Mariposa	San Diego	Sutter
Del Norte	Mendocino	San Francisco	Tehama
El Dorado	Merced	San Joaquin	Trinity
Fresno	Modoc	San Luis	Tulare
Glenn	Mono	Obispo	Tuolumne
Humboldt	Monterey	San Mateo	Ventura
Imperial	Napa	Santa Barbara	Yolo
Inyo	Nevada	Santa Clara	Yuba
Kern	Orange	Santa Cruz	

**WANTED.
YOUNG, SKINNY,
WIRY FELLOWS.
NOT OVER 18.
MUST BE
EXPERT
RIDERS.
WILLING TO
RISK DEATH
DAILY. ORPHANS
PREFERRED.**

Orphans Preferred

- Riders' pay was $100 per month.
- Mail cost $5 per half-ounce, but prices dropped and at the end it was $1 per half-ounce.
- In summer the average delivery took 10 days; in winter, from 12 to 16 days.
- Only one mailbag was ever lost; one rider died.

Although it only lasted sixteen months (from April 1860 to November 1861), the Pony Express demonstrated that a fast intercontinental mail service could operate year-round—something that had previously been thought impossible. Departing from St. Joseph, Missouri, routes went to Sacramento, San Diego, and other points in California. To this day, the Pony Express lives on in the popular imagination!

The youngest rider for the Pony Express was 11-year-old Charlie Miller. In those days, riders were paid three times what average workers made, and Charlie was a darn good rider. On July 11, 1861, "Broncho Charlie," as the other riders called him, rode out of Sacramento to Placerville and continued to ride for the next five months, until the service was shut down. Broncho Charlie met Bill Cody, another Pony Express rider, and later appeared in Buffalo Bill's Wild West show in the 1880s. He rode from New York to San Francisco to celebrate the 70th anniversary of the Pony Express—a long trip for an 81-year-old!

PONY EXPRESS TRIVIA

- Riders couldn't weigh more than 125 pounds.
- Stations were placed 10 miles apart—the maximum distance a horse can travel at full gallop.
- Riders changed every 75 to 100 miles—a full day's work at 10 mph!
- The invention of the telegraph caused the demise of the Pony Express.

The Golden Spike

Today it's hard for us to imagine not having a lot of ways to get from, say, St. Louis to Los Angeles or San Francisco. But less than 140 years ago, a covered wagon was your only option. Until the Central Pacific and Union Pacific Railroads joined forces to build the world's first transcontinental railroad. Sure, there were rail lines all over the place—but none crossed the Rockies until track was laid from Sacramento, California, to Omaha, Nebraska, in just six years. The two lines met in Promontory, Utah, on May 10, 1869.

- Sacramento, California, businessmen Leland Stanford, Collis Huntington, Charles Crocker, and Mark Hopkins financed the Central Pacific Railroad.
- At the ceremony to celebrate completion, a golden spike was driven into a polished California laurel tie. But pure gold would have been too soft, so the spike was actually alloyed with copper.
- After the ceremony, the laurel tie and golden spike were replaced with a regular iron spike and normal tie. The golden spike now resides in the Stanford Museum; the laurel tie was destroyed in the fires caused by the 1906 San Francisco earthquake.
- No Chinese were invited to the ceremony. Although it was held in Utah Territory, no Mormon officials were present either.
- East-west passengers still had to cross the Missouri River by boat until 1872, as no railroad bridge existed over the Missouri River between Council Bluffs, Iowa, and Omaha, Nebraska.

OK, EVERYBODY, NOW PUSH...

A powerful symbol not only of the city but of California, too, San Francisco's cable cars are the only street railway in the world that do not operate under their own power. Instead, there is a continuously moving steel cable running between the rails, kept in motion by an engine in a centrally located powerhouse. The car simply grips the cable and is dragged over its route.

- San Francisco is now the only city in the world to operate cable cars.
- When lines intersect, the car gripping the lower cable must let go, coast across the intersection, and pick up the cable again on the other side.
- Given the hilly nature of San Francisco streets, sometimes passengers have to help push a car to a point it can grip its cable.

Headed to LAX

Officially the Los Angeles International Airport—and originally known as Mines Field—LAX has been in use as an aviation field since 1928. Commercial flights started in 1946, and today LAX is the world's busiest airport, for passengers originating or arriving at an airport. This doesn't count passengers making connecting flights! In 2005, more than 61 million people traveled through the terminal in Los Angeles.

> The longest airplane runway in the world is 7.5 miles long, at Edwards Air Force Base in California. Among various test aircraft, the runway has been the landing point for several space shuttle missions.

The Right Stuff

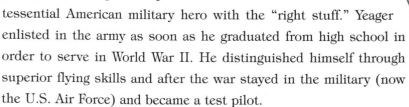

Immortalized in Tom Wolfe's book about the manned space program, Chuck Yeager is a quintessential American military hero with the "right stuff." Yeager enlisted in the army as soon as he graduated from high school in order to serve in World War II. He distinguished himself through superior flying skills and after the war stayed in the military (now the U.S. Air Force) and became a test pilot.

Yeager is most famous for test-flying the rocket-powered Bell X-1 and being the first to break the sound barrier in level flight on October 14, 1947, at an altitude of 45,000 feet. Afterwards it was revealed that he'd broken two ribs while horse riding two nights before the scheduled flight and had been in so much pain he was unable to seal the plane's hatch, so he'd used a broom handle as a lever. He'd gone to a veterinarian in a neighboring town to be treated.

Yeager went on to break many speed and altitude records out of Edwards Air Force Base in the western Mojave Desert. He flew for some thirty years after his retirement from the air force, and currently resides in Grass Valley, California.

> I was lucky to live through the thing, lucky to be involved. I was at the right place at the right time at the right age, and I had the right ... capability to take advantage of it.
>
> —CHUCK YEAGER

DRYDEN FLIGHT RESEARCH CENTER

Edwards Air Force Base is also home to Dryden Flight Research Center, NASA's primary site for aeronautical research; some of the most advanced—and often most secret—aircraft in the world are operated and tested at Dryden.

A CALIFORNIA ROAD TRIP!

Want to get a good look at what the Golden State has to offer? Hop in the car—and put the top down—for a California road trip vacation!

STOP #1: SAN DIEGO
Considered the birthplace of California, San Diego is the perfect place to start your trip. Just an hour from the border with Mexico, the city reflects its Spanish roots in architecture and cultural activities.
- visit the Mission Bay area to soak in the funky surfer culture
- take the kids to the world-famous zoo or SeaWorld
- ride the antique (1910) merry-go-round in Balboa Park
- check out the Maritime Museum
- take in a San Diego Chargers football game at Qualcomm Stadium

STOP #2: LOS ANGELES
Take I-5 up to Los Angeles, where you could easily spend a week just seeing the major sights! L.A. has an atmosphere all its own—enjoy!
- visit Hollywood: take a studio tour or see the stars' homes
- shop on Rodeo Drive in Beverly Hills
- spend a couple days at Disneyland
- admire the view from the Getty Museum
- stroll the UCLA and USC campuses
- sample the famous L.A. nightlife
- rollerblade on the Venice Beach boardwalk

STOP #3: SANTA BARBARA
The ocean breezes cool this beautiful oceanside city on Highway 101, in the heart of Southern California's wine country. You'll never want to leave ...
- check out the world-class Museum of Art
- spend a day at the Botanic Garden (bring a picnic lunch!)
- visit Stearns Wharf, then on East Beach soak up the sun
- take the Red Tile walking tour through historic S.B.
- sample the wineries on Foxen Canyon Trail

STOP #4: CARMEL
Follow historic Highway 1 up the majestic California coastline, and be sure to take every scenic overlook break! On the way visit Hearst Castle in San Simeon.
- spend a day hiking in Big Sur; stay for the sunset
- take the world-famous "17-Mile Drive"
- follow a golf tournament at Pebble Beach
- shop the dozens of boutiques and specialty shops on Ocean Avenue
- visit the world-famous Monterey Bay Aquarium

Sea cliffs in Carme

STOP #5: SAN FRANCISCO

Stay on Highway 1 around Monterey Bay as you head north; on your way, make a stop in Santa Cruz and enjoy its famous boardwalk and beaches. If you want, stop at beautiful Half Moon Bay before heading into the city where you will leave your heart!

- enjoy California cuisine (or any other) at four-star restaurants all over town
- take in a S.F. Giants baseball game—or the world-famous S.F. ballet
- walk through the city's distinct neighborhoods, including Chinatown (the largest outside Asia)
- drive down Lombard Street—the crookedest street in the world!
- be sure to ride the cable cars
- don't miss the world-class Museum of Modern Art

STOP #6: SONOMA

On your way out of town, drive across the magnificent Golden Gate Bridge and take Highway 101 north to the California wine country.

- enjoy Sonoma's historic downtown square, with boutiques, museums, and trendy restaurants
- visit the last Spanish mission on the Mission Trail
- spend the day at the nearby Luther Burbank Home and Gardens
- take a hot-air balloon ride over the wine country
- plan several days for wine-tasting at the dozens of local wineries

STOP #7: SACRAMENTO

Head east to the state's capital, a happy blend of old (it was the final stop on the Transcontinental Railroad) and new (Sacramento is one of the top ten fastest growing metropolitan areas in the country).

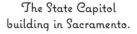

The State Capitol building in Sacramento.

- be sure to visit the State Capitol building, museum, and governor's mansion
- take a walking tour of Old Sacramento; see pioneer gravesites in the City Cemetery
- see Sutter's Fort, the center of the California Gold Rush; drive Highway 49 through mining country
- don't miss the Crocker Art Museum—or the State Railroad Museum!
- go whitewater rafting on the Sacramento or American Rivers

STOP #8: REDDING

Jump on I-5 and drive north toward Redding—although you're really heading for the Shasta Lake area, the largest man-made reservoir in California.

- rent a houseboat to explore Shasta Lake; fish all day!
- be sure to visit Shasta Dam: the second largest and highest in the nation
- walk the Sundial Bridge at Turtle Bay (yes, it tells time too!)
- visit Lassen Volcanic National Park
- tour local waterfalls, including Whiskeytown, Crystal Creek, and Brandy Creek

FOLLOW THE MISSION CHAIN

When Father Junipero Serra established the first mission in San Diego in 1769, he was the first non–Native American to live in the territory—and he changed the face of California forever. A steady stream of Dominicans, Jesuits, and Franciscans arrived to establish the 21 missions along the coast, introducing European livestock and plants—and European diseases that were often devastating for the local residents.

Traveling from south to north from San Diego to Sonoma the missions are as follows (chronological order):

San Diego de Alcala (1) / 1769
San Luis Rey de Francia (18) / 1798
San Juan Capistrano (7) / 1776
San Gabriel Arcangel (4) / 1771
San Buenaventura (9) / 1782
San Fernando Rey de Espana (17) / 1797
Santa Barbara (10) / 1786
Santa Ines (19) / 1804
La Purisima Conception (11) / 1787
San Luis Obispo de Tolosa (5) / 1772
San Miguel Arcangel (16) / 1797
San Antonia de Padua (3) / 1771
Nuestra Senora de la Soledad (13) / 1791
San Carlos Borromeo de Carmelo (2) 1770
San Juan Bautista (15) / 1797
Santa Cruz (12) / 1791
Santa Clara de Asis (8) / 1777
San Jose (14) / 1797
San Francisco de Asis, Mission Dolores (6) 1776
San Rafael Arcangel (20) / 1817
San Francisco Solano (21) / 1823

Mission San Juan Capistrano / 1776
Considered one of the most beautiful of the mission ruins, the Serra Chapel is the oldest building still in use in California and the only surviving church where Father Serra said mass.
Ortega Hwy. at Camino Capistrano, San Juan Capistrano, 92693, (949) 248-2049

Mission San Juan Capistrano.

Mission MishMash

• Mission San Buenaventura was the last mission founded by Father Serra personally.

• Indians repeatedly shot flaming arrows into the roof of Mission San Luis Obispo, so the fathers tiled it instead—an idea that caught on at all the missions!

• Mission San Carlos in Carmel was Father Serra's favorite and his headquarters; he is buried here.

• Want to have a wedding at Mission San Diego? You'll need to schedule it at least nine months in advance.

• Over 25,000 baptisms were conducted at Mission San Gabriel between 1771 and 1834, making it the most prolific in the mission chain.

• San Juan Capistrano is famous for being the summer home of the Argentinian cliff swallows; their return each March is celebrated with a fiesta.

• The water treatment system at Mission Santa Barbara—all built by Native American Indian labor—was so extraordinary that parts of it are still used by the city of Santa Barbara.

• The Mission San Juan Bautista and its grounds were featured prominently in the 1958 Paramount Pictures film **Vertigo**, starring Jimmy Stewart.

• Earthquakes destroyed Mission Santa Cruz; now a half-size replica exists on the site.

• Mission Santa Barbara is only mission to remain under the leadership of the Franciscan friars since the day of its founding, continuously serving as the parish church.

• Mission San Francisco in Sonoma was the site of the Bear Flag Revolt in 1846.

• No town grew up around Mission San Antonio; perhaps this is why this mission is said to be the closest to original condition.

• Hostile, native Indians were so moved by a painting of "Our Lady" that they immediately made peace with the priests who built Mission San Gabriel; the painting still hangs in the sanctuary.

• The original murals at Mission San Miguel are today the best preserved in California.

• Mission Santa Clara was the first California mission named for a woman.

Santa Barbara Mission

• The isolated Mission Nuestra Senora de la Soledad was restored in the 1950s and still uses the original tile floor.

HOORAY FOR HOLLYWOOD

SEE A (FIRST-RUN) MOVIE IN A SPECTACULAR MOVIE PALACE

Cinerama Dome: 6360 Sunset Blvd., Hollywood / (323) 464-4226

El Capitan: 6838 Hollywood Blvd., Hollywood 90028 /
(323) 467-7674 or (323) 467-9545

Grauman's Chinese Theatre: 6925 Hollywood Blvd., Hollywood
90028 / (323) 464-8111 or (323) 461-3331

Grauman's Egyptian: 6712 Hollywood Blvd., Hollywood 90028 /
(323) 466-3456

Mann Village Theater: 961 Broxton, Westwood 90024 / (310)
248-6266

Nuart Theatre: 11272 Santa Monica Blvd., W. Los Angeles 90025
(310) 281-8223

Westwood Crest Theater: 1262 Westwood Blvd., Westwood 90024
(310) 474-7866

VISIT CLASSIC HOLLYWOOD ATTRACTIONS (SOME CHEESY, SOME NOT SO MUCH!)

Guinness World Record Museum: 6764 Hollywood Blvd.,
Hollywood 90028 / (323) 462-5991 or (323) 463-6433

Hollywood Entertainment Museum: 7021 Hollywood Blvd.,
Hollywood 90028 / (323) 465-7900

Hollywood Heritage Museum (DeMille Barn): 2100 N. Highland Blvd., Hollywood 90028 / (323) 874-2276 or (323) 874-4005

Hollywood Museum: 1660 N. Highland Ave., Hollywood 90028 / (323) 464 7776

Kodak Theater: 6801 Hollywood Blvd., Hollywood 90028 / (323) 308-6300

Museum of Television and Radio: 465 N. Beverly Dr., Beverly Hills 90210 / (310) 786-1025

Ripley's Believe It Or Not: 6780 Hollywood Blvd., Hollywood 90028 / (323) 466-6335

Warner Bros. Museum: 3400 Riverside Dr., Burbank 91522 / (818) 972-8687

TAKE A STUDIO TOUR

Warner Bros. Studio: 4000 Warner Blvd., Burbank 91505 / (818) 954-1744 or (818) 954-1008

M-G-M (now Sony Pictures): 10202 W. Washington Blvd., Culver City 90232 / (310) 280-8000

Paramount Studios: 5555 Melrose Ave., Hollywood 90232 / (323) 956-5575

Universal Studios: 100 Universal City Plaza (at Lankershim), Universal City 91608 / (818) 508-9600 or (818) 508-5444

NBC Studios: 3000 W. Alameda Ave., Burbank / (818) 840-3537 or (818) 840-4444

CHECK OUT LOCAL LANDMARKS

Bonaventure Hotel: 404 S. Figueroa Street, Los Angeles 90071 / (213) 624-1000

Built in 1976, this futuristic landmark has appeared in more than one science fiction movie—including Blade Runner *and* Strange Days. *Definitely worth a drive-by!*

Capitol Records Building: 1750 N. Vine St., Hollywood 90028 / (323) 871-5003

Built in 1954, the first record company located on the West Coast makes its headquarters in the world's first circular office building. Does it look like a stack of records? You be the judge.

The Hollywood Bowl: 2301 Highland Ave., Hollywood 90078 / (323) 850-2058

The world's largest natural amphitheater, built in 1919, has been the site of a host of renowned concerts (think Beatles) and featured in movies too. Just blocks from Hollywood Boulevard.

Hollywood Memorial Cemetery: 6000 Santa Monica Blvd., Hollywood 90038 / (323) 469-1181

Maps are available to locate famous stars' graves such as Douglas Fairbanks and Edward G. Robinson.

Hollywood Sign: Mount Lee, Griffith Park, Los Angeles 90027

One of the city's most recognizable landmarks, the sign is visible from many locations. It has been featured in films, the victim of pranks, and imitated around the world.

Shrine Auditorium: 649 W. Jefferson Blvd., Los Angeles 90007 / (213) 749-5123

The largest indoor auditorium in the U.S., this opera house is often the home of the annual Academy Awards show.

Tower Records on the Sunset Strip: 8801 Sunset Blvd., West Hollywood 90069 / (310) 657-7300

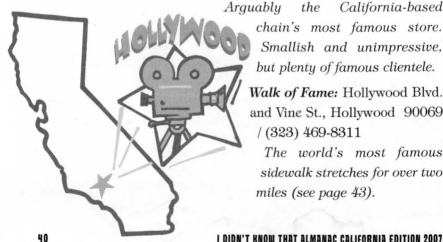

Arguably the California-based chain's most famous store. Smallish and unimpressive, but plenty of famous clientele.

Walk of Fame: Hollywood Blvd. and Vine St., Hollywood 90069 / (323) 469-8311

The world's most famous sidewalk stretches for over two miles (see page 43).

Walking Hollywood

Broadway, in downtown Los Angeles, boasts a collection of '20s and '30s movie palaces with spectacular façade architecture and even more spectacular interiors. Sadly, many are now shuttered (or they've become churches or swap-meets), but you can take a guided walking tour offered by the Los Angeles Conservancy. They recommend that you make reservations for the tour a month in advance. Call (213) 623-2489.

On some summer mornings (usually Tuesdays, Thursdays, and Fridays), rehearsals at the Hollywood Bowl are open to the public (free)! Call (323) 850-2000 for information.

It's illegal to hike to or get anywhere near the Hollywood sign. A 1993 incident in which UCLA students altered the sign to read GO UCLA before a football game was the final straw, prompting the city to install a $100,000 security system, complete with video surveillance and motion detection. The official Web site (**www.hollywoodsign.org**) suggests several places from which to take great photographs, though!

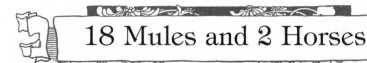

18 Mules and 2 Horses

When borax was discovered near what was then known as Furnace Creek Ranch, it birthed an industry that is important to this day. (Borax is used in detergents, water softeners, and enamel glazes, among other industrial uses.) Although several companies were mining borax in Death Valley at the end of the nineteenth century, just one remains: the twenty-mule team company now known simply as Borax. It operates the largest open-pit mine in California and supplies almost half of the world's borates needs. And although that original marketing campaign still resonates, the fact of the matter is it was really eighteen mules and two horses pulling those ten-ton wagons!

Amargosa Opera House

In the tiny ghost town (once a borax mining company town) of Death Valley Junction, where there are no restaurants and no gas stations, there *is* an opera house. Founded by Marta Becket, this beautiful opera house came to life when the

professional dancer and her husband vacationed nearby and discovered the deserted movie theater.

Outside a Mexican colonial style building, inside the walls are painted with elaborate murals—an entire sixteenth-century audience just waiting for Marta's next performance. The first performance was for a live audience of twelve in 1968. Today Marta performs a dance and pantomime show—with many costume changes—for lively audiences who come from miles and miles away. Some stay in the small hotel attached to the opera house. Shows begin promptly at 8:15 PM.

A GRAND TRADITION

In 1958 the city of Los Angeles wanted to give Hollywood a facelift—and an enduring tradition was born. For over two miles along Hollywood Boulevard and Vine Street, the charcoal-grey terrazzo sidewalk is embedded with pink granite stars featuring the names of celebrities honored by the Hollywood Chamber of Commerce for their contributions to the entertainment industry.

WHAT THE EMBLEMS MEAN:

Television set = contributions to broadcast television
Radio microphone = contributions to broadcast radio
Comedy/Tragedy masks = contributions to live theater/performance
Motion picture camera = contributions to the movie industry
Phonograph record = contributions to the recording industry

Did You Know?

John Lennon's star on the Hollywood Walk of Fame is right outside the Capitol Records building, and is often the site of candlelight vigils on the anniversary of his death (December 8).

Q: How many nominations are submitted to the Hollywood Chamber each year?
A: The committee receives an average of two hundred applications a year.

The first Hollywood Walk of Fame star was awarded to Joanne Woodward on February 9, 1960. As of April 2006, there have been 2,309 stars awarded.

Gene Autry is the only person to have been honored with five stars—one in each category!

The criteria for a star on the walk of fame is: 1) Professional achievement; 2) Longevity of five years in the field of entertainment; and 3) Contributions to the community. In addition, the recipient must agree to attend the dedication ceremony.

SEE AND BE SEEN
50 GREAT NIGHTSPOTS TO SEE STARS

Put on your high-heeled shoes and head out for a night on the town—and maybe you'll run into a celebrity or two. Remember that trends and tastes do change, though—trying to predict the latest hot spot is like trying to predict the next earthquake.

A.D. / 836 N. HIGHLAND AVE., LOS ANGELES 90038 / (323) 467-3000
With some of the best DJ talent on the West Coast, this elegant dance club has more than one lounge in a building modeled after a medieval castle. Use valet: parking is scarce. Popular with celebrities.

Buffalo Club / 1520 OLYMPIC BLVD., SANTA MONICA 90404 / (310) 450-8600
The glitterati love this upscale cocktail lounge with both indoor and out-door spaces. Dress to kill and expect to wait behind the velvet rope.

Catalina Bar & Grill / 6725 W. Sunset Blvd., Los Angeles 90028 / (323) 466-2210
This well-known jazz club attracts A-list acts and A-list patrons too. Be sure to make reservations, as the club is small and popular.

Chaya's / 110 NAVY ST., VENICE 90291 / (310) 396-1179
The bar in this popular restaurant offers superlative specialty cocktails and excellent celebrity watching!

Lava Lounge / 1533 LA BREA AVE., HOLLYWOOD 90028 / (323) 876-6612
Don't be put off by the strip mall location—this warm, cozy bar with tiki lounge décor attracts the Hollywood crowd and is a great value besides, with half-price drinks from 8:30 to 10:00 PM.

The Polo Lounge at the Beverly Hills Hotel / 9641 SUNSET BLVD., BEVERLY HILLS 90210 / (310) 276-2251
Aside from the fact that it will be packed with Hollywood A-listers, the Polo Lounge is a must-see just to soak in the Hollywood history.

RokBar / 11710 N. LAS PALMAS AVE., HOLLYWOOD 90028 / (323) 461-5600
Investors in this swank Hollywood club include rocker Tommy Lee and DJ sensation Paul Oakenfold—and the club sports a laid-back, rock-n-roll attitude. Plenty of Hollywood folks have been here too.

Roof Bar @The Standard / 550 S. FLOWER ST., LOS ANGELES 90071 / (213) 892-8080
This chic poolside bar atop the ultrahip Standard Hotel has a glorious nighttime view of the L.A. skyline.

Skybar / 8440 SUNSET BLVD., W. HOLLYWOOD 90069 / (323) 848-6025
The pool area at the modernist Mondrian Hotel becomes a cocktail party after dark; to get in, book a room or show up before 8:00 PM.

Spago / 176 N. CAÑON DR., BEVERLY HILLS 90210 / (310) 385-0880
You know about the restaurant, but Spago is a great place for drinks too—and the celebrity sightings are first-rate!

The Standard / 8300 W. SUNSET BLVD., W. HOLLYWOOD 90069 / (323) 650-9090
This chic hotel offers two outstanding clubs (the other is Roof Bar); this lounge features an all-purple, dim, and intimate experience. Expect to see celebrities having a quiet drink while they enjoy a scenic view of the L.A. basin.

The Troubadour / 9081 SANTA MONICA BLVD., W. HOLLYWOOD 90069 / (310) 276-6168
This Los Angeles landmark has managed to stay hip by changing with the times—and still features great acts. Plenty of celebrity sightings too.

The Viper Room / 8852 SUNSET BLVD., W. HOLLYWOOD 90069 / (310) 358-1880
Celebrity sightings are common here, thanks to the dark, ultrahip atmosphere and great live music.

A LAUGH A MINUTE

Hollywood is an entertainer's town—and comedy clubs are a great place to be entertained!

• THE COMEDY STORE
8433 Sunset Blvd., W. Hollywood 90069 / (323) 656-6225

It was a good year for comedy, 1972 ... Comedians Sammy Shore and Rudy DeLuca opened the Comedy Store on the Sunset Strip in April; Johnny Carson moved the *Tonight Show* west in May, effectively relocating the center of the stand-up world from New York; and Richard Pryor staged his "comeback" at the fledgling comedy club in June. And things took off from there. By the fall of '79, the club was such a success that the inaugural HBO Young Comedians Special was filmed here.

• THE IMPROV
8162 Melrose Ave., W. Hollywood 90069 / (323) 651-2583

Establishing an outpost from its New York location (founded in 1963), the Hollywood Improv opened in 1974 and has flourished ever since, providing a home for plenty of comedy royalty. Eddie Murphy started out at the Improv when he was only 16 years old; Jim Carrey started at 19—and bombed in his first appearance.

• THE LAUGH FACTORY
8001 Sunset Blvd., W. Hollywood 90069 / (323) 656-1336

Founder Jamie Masada arrived in Hollywood in 1977, broke, alone, speaking only Farsi, and just 14 years old. His dream of becoming a comic did not come true, but Masada has built a comedy empire through hard work—and by giving back the compassion that was shown to him along the way. Ever an innovator—he was the first to actually pay comedians, in an era when most performed just for the exposure—Masada also was a champion of diversity and crossover promotion too. This legendary comedy club (in a landmark building that once was the offices of the Marx Brothers) always has a line outside, and with good reason: you'll see today's hottest comics as well as the most promising up-and-coming stars in quality shows.

Hot & HOTTER

California is blessed with a multitude of natural hot springs ... just the thing for relaxing. Many are "primitive"—in remote areas, with no improvements added (and therefore require no fees), while others have amenities and improvements, or even resorts. Here is a sampling of each for your enjoyment. Do note that at many primitive sites, clothing is optional.

Primitive

- **Buckeye Hot Spring (Central California)**

Northeast of Yosemite near Bridgeport, this spring cascades over a large rock before pooling beside Buckeye Creek. Just off Highway 395, eight miles northwest of Bridgeport in the Toiyabe National Forest.

- **Eagleville Hot Spring (Northern California)**

Near Cedarville in the northeast corner of the state, just off Surprise Valley Road. You'll have to walk down a steep incline—but it's worth it. Stop in Cedarville for directions.

- **Little Caliente / Big Caliente Hot Springs (Southern California)**

Located in Los Padres National Forest north of Santa Barbara and accessible by dirt roads, these hot springs are isolated and uncrowded. There are camping facilities near Big Caliente; check with the park station (or online) for directions.

Basic Amenities

- **Orr Hot Springs (Northern California)**

Not far from Ukiah in a wooded valley with fantastic scenery, this rustic resort has a communal kitchen, some campsites and cabins, a hostel-type dormitory, and public bathrooms.

- **Sam's Family Spa (Southern California)**

With a small hotel and plenty of camp-

> ### HOT SPRINGS TIPS
> - Watch your step; footing can be slippery.
> - Don't go alone.
> - Test the temperature first.
> - Respect private property: ask first.
> - Don't drink the water.

grounds, this unpretentious resort is located in Desert Hot Springs, just twelve miles from Palm Springs.

- **Wilbur Hot Springs Resort (Northern California)**

Boasting a historic Victorian hotel (some private rooms, some dormitory-style), and a few campsites, this hot springs near Williams is in the middle of a nature preserve.

Let Us Entertain You!

Tourism is one of California's top four industries, and these terrific amusement parks have a lot to do with that!

DISNEYLAND® RESORT

1313 S. Harbor Blvd.; Anaheim, CA 92803-3232 / (714) 781-4565

The granddaddy of them all (it opened in 1955), this kingdom truly is magic. There are eight fantastic lands here, from nostalgic Main Street USA to Tomorrowland, with so much excitement in between it would take several days to see it all. And that's just the one park—right next door is Disney's California Adventure (for an older audience, it has a California theme, including a miniature Golden Gate Bridge) and Downtown Disney, an outdoor shopping, dining, and entertainment area, with three hotels. Both areas opened in 2001, and, taken as a whole, the three areas comprise what's now called the

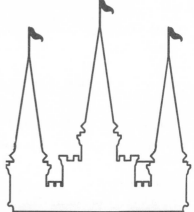

Disneyland has been closed only twice: the first due to the assassination of JFK in November 1963 and the second on September 11, 2001.

Disneyland Resort. Every kid wants to go to Disneyland, and every adult regains the best part of childhood when in the park—come see for yourself!

And That's Not All, Folks!

Here are more fun attractions for the whole family!

- Pacific Park / 380 Santa Monica Pier, Santa Monica 90401 / (310) 260-8744
- Paramount's Great America / 4701 Great America Pkwy., Santa Clara 95054 / (408) 988-1776 x8858
- Raging Waters / 2333 South White Rd., San Jose 95148 / (408) 238-9900
- Raging Waters / 111 Raging Waters Dr., San Dimas 91773 / (909) 802-2200
- Santa Cruz Beach Boardwalk / 400 Beach St., Santa Cruz 95060 / (831) 423-5590
- Sea World / 500 SeaWorld Dr., San Diego 92109 / (800) 25-SHAMU
- Six Flags Marine World / 2001 Marine World Pkwy., Vallejo 94589 / (707) 643-6722

KNOTT'S BERRY FARM

8039 Beach Blvd.; Buena Park, CA 90620 / (714) 220-5200

They aren't kidding—this well-established theme park (it opened in 1968) started in the 1920s as a family roadside stand out in front of Walter Knott's berry farm. After wife Cordelia opened an immensely popular fried chicken restaurant, Walter built a little ghost town out back to entertain folks as they waited for a table. One thing led to another, and before long the Knotts were charging admission to this charming, rustic attraction now known for its several large roller coasters, including the much-acclaimed GhostRider, an authentic wooden roller coaster. With a variety of themed areas that will please all ages, Knott's Berry Farm is more fun than a bushel of, well, berries. What's more—the famous Knott's Chicken Dinner Restaurant's still open!

LEGOLAND®

One LEGOLAND Dr.
Carlsbad, CA 92008 / (760) 918-5346

What will they think of next? The landscape at LEGOLAND is just plain cool, with models of famous buildings and replicas of famous scenes—including an impressive New York City skyline—created from literally millions of the tiny plastic blocks, thus living up to their stated theme: Where Creativity Meets Fun. Although the park is specially geared to kids aged two to twelve, and has such attractions as the LEGO Mindstorms Center (fun-based learning activities), Explore Village, Knight's Kingdom, and Imagination Zone, as well as numerous rides for the very short, there's plenty here for moms and dads too—aside from the sheer pleasure of knowing that they themselves did not have to assemble any of the LEGO projects on the property! Didn't get enough of the LEGO experience? Stop by Fun Town to stock up on bulk LEGO bricks, purchased by the pound!

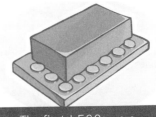

The first LEGOs were wooden, made in Ole Kirk Christiansen's small workshop in Billund, Denmark, in 1932; in 1949 the first plastic LEGOs were introduced. Christiansen called his toys **LEGO** from a contraction of the Danish words **leg godt**, meaning "play well." It was later learned that LEGO in Latin means "I put together" or "I assemble"!

BEATING THE FRENCH AT THEIR OWN GAME

There was a time when California wines "got no respect"—but no more!

The first vintner in California was Father Junipero Serra—in fact, he's called "the Father of California Wine"—as he oversaw the planting of a vineyard at Mission San Diego in 1769 (he went on to establish eight more missions with vineyards before his death in 1784). The first known European vines were imported by a Frenchman, Jean-Louis Vignes, in 1833, but it took Agoston Harazsthy, a Hungarian soldier, to found the California wine industry that we know today. A man of boundless enthusiasm, Harazsthy traveled back and forth to Europe (at his own expense and with grants from the state) in the 1850s and '60s, bringing cuttings from 165 of Europe's greatest wineries and establishing them in Northern California. He opened Buena Vista Winery in Sonoma in 1857.

By the turn of the century, the quality of California wines had reached excellence by international standards, evidenced by the many medals won by them at the 1900 Paris Exposition—including the Grand Prize, awarded to a claret from Liparita Winery in the Napa Valley. Prohibition nearly killed the fledgling California industry; production dropped 94 percent between 1919 and the national repeal in 1933, … and the fact that most growers had switched from fine wine grapes to juice grapes stunted what was left until the early 1970s. California wines were sneered at by the established European community.

Fast-forward to 1976. A blind tasting was held in Paris, with judges made up of French wine experts, and the results shook the world of winemaking: of the top four Chardonnays, three were Californian; the top red wine also was born in the Golden State. Ten years later, the same wines were tested again, and the California wines improved their rankings, having aged better than their French counterparts; in 2006 the same wines again improved their rankings, capturing the top five of ten spots! Sneered at no longer, California wines grace the most sophisticated tables in the world.

Whole volumes have been written about the fruit of the vine ... and educated wine tasting can take years of practice (although we certainly don't mind the homework!). But a little bit of knowledge can go a long way toward enhancing your enjoyment of the experience.

First rule: Don't be intimidated by the vast array to choose from in the liquor store. Ask the store clerk or another shopper for suggestions. Some folks follow the grape harvest the way others follow the stock market—while the rest of us are doing other things. Most wine aficionados love to talk about their passion, though, so ask!

Grapes: Varieties of grapes—pinot noir, chardonnay, or merlot, for example—often lend their names to the name of the wine, according to the percentage of that grape use in the mix (defined by law as a minimum of 75 or 85 percent). These are called varietal wines. Blended wines are also popular (they just go by other names).

Classifying wines: Wines are classified in several ways, including vinification methods (sparkling, still, fortified, rosé, blush), taste (dry, sweet), vintage (the year the grapes were harvested), wine style (often named for the region the grapes were grown in), vineyard, and by quality.

The color of wine is not determined by the juice of the grape, but by whether or not the grape skins were present during fermentation.

Tasting wine: Tasting wine involves three senses—sight, smell, and taste...

SIGHT: Wine should be clear and bright, not cloudy or hazy

SMELL: Swirl a half-glass of wine in the glass, then smell it. Your nose is more sensitive than your palate, so don't miss the opportunity to appreciate this experience.

TASTE: Swish that first mouthful around to get the full affect. Don't forget to notice the aftertaste too.

Now go out and buy a few bottles of California wine to celebrate your graduation!

Come, brothers, hurry, I am drinking stars!
—DOM PÉRIGNON

Contrary to popular belief, Dom Pérignon (a French monk), did not invent champagne—although he did have a lot to do with advances made in its production. No one knows how it was invented, actually. But who cares? This heavenly, bubbly wine—sometimes called sparkling wine outside the Champagne region of France—is perfect anytime.

• Champagne is made from a mixture of grapes, not a single grape as many wines are.

• The three traditional champagne grapes are chardonnay, pinot noir, and meunieur.

• Cuvée simply means "blend."

• Champagne ranges from sweet to dry (not sweet!); the names for this are doux, demi-sec, sec, extra-dry, brut, extra brut.

• It takes about 1,150 grapes to make a single bottle of champagne.

• Champagne ferments twice: first in barrels, then in bottles.

• After champagne is bottled, it is aged for 18 months to 3 years.

• Champagne bottles are rotated a little each day (called riddling) and moved to a neck-down position so sediment can be easily removed (called disgorgement).

• There are approximately 58 million bubbles in one bottle of champagne.

• The pressure in a bottle of champagne is 90 pounds per square inch—about three times that in your automobile tire.

• Corks can exit the bottle at 38–40 mph, so be careful!

GETTING SIDEWAYS

Old friends Miles and Jack take a trip through the Santa Barbara area wine country to celebrate Jack's upcoming wedding in the 2005 movie *Sideways.* Eighteen wineries, innumerable wines, and the gorgeous Santa Barbara countryside play supporting roles in this hilarious movie about friendship, fading youth, and facing the future. The Santa Barbara Conference & Visitors Bureau and Film Commission even offers a self-guided tour map featuring actual wineries and restaurants Miles and Jack visited: just call (805) 966-9222.

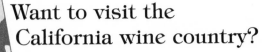

Want to visit the California wine country?

With so many winemaking districts to choose from, you could stay busy for weeks! Here are a few recommendations.

Napa Valley: Widely considered one of the top districts in the country, it is also one of the oldest. There are more than 140 wineries here, and the area is very popular, so expect crowds, or come in the winter. Look for great cabernet sauvignons and chardonnays. We recommend: Beringer, Clos Pegase, Robert Mondavi, Sterling, Sutter Home, and V. Sattui wineries.

Sonoma Valley: The birthplace of the California wine industry, Sonoma is home to several historic wineries—and the scenery here is spectacular. Try cabernet sauvignon, chardonnay, merlot, zinfandel, pinot noir, and sauvignon blanc. We recommend: Benziger, Buena Vista, Ferrari-Carano, Korbel, Ravenswood, St. Francis, Silver Oak, and Viansa wineries.

Santa Barbara County: Although only two hours' drive from Los Angeles, the rural setting feels like another world entirely. The ocean breezes add something special to the wine here too. Great pinot noir and syrah. We recommend: Andrew Murray, Bridlewood, Cambria, Firestone, Rancho Sisquoc, Sanford, and Sunstone wineries.

Sierra Foothills: Beautiful country in historic gold mining area, and hardly ever crowded, this area boasts several small, interesting wineries. This is zinfandel country. We recommend: Cedarville, Fitzpatrick, Latcham, Mount Aukum, Oakstone, and Windwalker wineries.

As a rule, grapevines prefer a relatively long growing season of one hundred days or more with warm daytime temperatures (no greater than 95°F) and cool nights (a difference of 40°F or more).

WHEN SHOULD I VISIT THE WINE COUNTRY?

It depends on what your priorities are, of course, but we think every time's a good time to visit! Here are some general guidelines.

December, January: Looking for peace and quiet? Avoid the traffic and crowds with a visit before the vineyard staff gets busy too.

February: It's still quiet, but spring comes early and the wildflowers are beginning to bloom. Bring your camera.

March, April: Wildflowers have gone crazy, and now the vines are coming back to life too. Temperatures are moderate, making this heaven on earth.

May–July: The grapevines are at their most magnificent, with lots of greenery and the grapes showing through. It's hot, and there are crowds at the most popular locations, especially on weekends.

August: Hot, dry, and crowded—but the grapes on the vine are a thing of beauty and the expectation of the harvest gives every winery an air of excitement.

September, October: It's harvest time (depending on climate and region), and the vineyard staff is very busy. Large crowds come to get a first look at the grape crush. Call ahead: some wineries may limit their tour times because they're so busy.

November: The vines and trees put on a spectacular fall display (don't forget your camera!), and weekends can still be busy, but the weather's quite pleasant!

Non-Snobs Guide to Choosing Wine

	Delicate	Hearty, earthy	Spicy, pungent
Flavors are	Delicate	Hearty, earthy	Spicy, pungent
Herbs used	Rosemary, dill, cinnamon, garlic	Oregano, clove, mustard, sage, ginger	Basil, parsley, nutmeg, anise
Sauces served	Lemon glaze	Cream, butter	Wine-based, meat sauce
Cheeses are	Bleu, goat, gorgonzola	Mozzarella, feta, cheddar gruyere, ricotta, pecorino	Camembert, brie
Foods include	Fish, salads, vegetables	Pork, poultry, veal	Red meat
Preparation	Steamed, poached	Roasted, baked, sauteed	Braised, grilled
Try This Wine...			
Type	Sauvignon blanc, riesling	Sangiovese, merlot, chardonnay, pinot noir	Cabernet sauvignon, zinfandel, syrah

Source: www.foxsearchlight.com/sideways

This Venice Isn't Sinking

Once known as the Coney Island of the Pacific, Venice was incorporated as a beach resort in 1905, complete with manmade canals to imitate that other Venice. Soon it boasted a huge entertainment pier with roller coasters, although Disneyland other nearby amusement parks eventually caused its decline. The focus of the Muscle Beach crowd in the '40s and '50s, and the roller-skate craze in the '70s and '80s, Venice has a quirky personality and a vibrant beachfront. But wait! There's more...

• Venice was annexed by Los Angeles in 1925—but it keeps threatening to secede!

• *The Lawrence Welk Show* got its start at the Aragon Ballroom in Venice.

• The Venice Family Clinic is the largest free clinic in the U.S.

• Most of the canals were filled in to make way for the automobile; however, there are still a few.

• Venice was the first home of Carroll Shelby's Mustang modification company.

• The Doors got their start in 1960s Venice.

• The 1978 movie *Grease* was filmed at Venice High School.

• Venice is the headquarters of the L.A. County Lifeguard Division of the Fire Department, the nation's largest ocean lifeguard organization.

More California Trivia

• The only Taco Bell restaurant located directly on a beach is in Pacifica.

• San Francisco's cable cars are the only national monument that moves!

• For 40 years there was a lone phone booth in the Mojave Desert, 15 miles from the nearest road; it received dozens of calls per day.

In the Middle of Nowhere!

Scotty's Castle—its real name is Death Valley Ranch—is a huge Spanish-style villa now owned and operated as a living museum by the National Park Service—complete with park rangers dressed in period clothing. The home is named for Death Valley Scotty, a con man who sold shares in a gold mine that never produced, but who managed to forge a friendship with the last person he swindled—Chicago millionaire Albert Johnson. When the ailing Johnson visited Death Valley, his health improved so much in the dry climate that he began bringing his wife for visits. It was Mrs. Johnson who suggested building something a little more comfortable than tents!

Thus began nine years of construction on a home that was built with cutting-edge technology (for 1922)—there are over a quarter mile of tunnels underneath the mansion that allow access to the workings of the house, including a water wheel that generated electricity. Sadly, a land dispute ended the building before the home was finished (there are thousands of tiles in the basement for a swimming pool that was never built). But the home is just as it was when the Johnsons lived there—filled with custom-made furniture and wrought-iron, European antiques, and a 1,121-pipe Welte theater organ.

Scotty's Castle is open year-round for tours; for more information, call (760) 786-2392 extension 224.

Did You Know...

The Academy of Motion Picture Arts and Sciences has nominated at least one alumnus of the University of Southern California each year since the inception of the Academy Awards in 1929!

You KNOW You're in California When...

You were born somewhere else.

You make over $250,000 a year and you STILL can't afford a house.

The fastest part of your commute is down your driveway.

The three-hour traffic jam you just sat through wasn't caused by a horrific nine-car pile-up, but by rubbernecking at a lost shoe lying on the shoulder.

You drive to your neighborhood block party.

A really great parking space can move you to tears.

Your neighbors, a family of four, own six vehicles.

It's sprinkling outside and the lead story on every news station is "Storm Watch '07."

You're not alarmed by the shaking.

You pack shorts and a T-shirt for the mountains, and a sweater and a wetsuit for the beach.

Your children learn to walk in Birkenstocks.

Your third-grader's teacher has purple hair, a nose ring, and is named Breeze.

Your best friends just named their twins after her acting coach and his personal trainer.

Your cat has its own psychiatrist.

You'll reluctantly miss yoga class to wait for the hot tub repairman.

You're thinking of taking an adult class but you can't decide between aromatherapy and conversational Mandarin.

You know how to eat an artichoke.

A glass has been reserved for you at your favorite winery.

You know which restaurant serves the freshest arugula.

That guy in line at Starbucks wearing the baseball cap and sunglasses who looks like George Clooney IS George Clooney.

Ahead of the Pack

Although the federal government enacted the Endangered Species Act in 1973, the state of California was way out ahead of the pack when it comes to protecting its native wildlife. In the 1960s, lists were created of animals that were rare or faced extinction, and these species were referenced as "Fully Protected." To this day, according to the Department of Fish and Game, "Fully Protected species may not be taken or possessed at any time and no licenses or permits may be issued for their take except for collecting these species for necessary scientific research and relocation of the bird species for the protection of livestock." Here is the complete Fully Protected list of birds and mammals:

BIRDS

American peregrine falcon (*Falco peregrinus anatum*)
Bald eagle (*Haliaeetus leucocephalus*)
California black rail (*Laterallus jamaicensis coturniculus*)
California brown pelican (*Pelecanus occidentalis*)
California clapper rail (*Rallus longirostris obsoletus*)
California condor (*Gymnogyps califonianus*)
California least tem (*Sterna antillarum browni*)
Golden eagle (*Aquila chrysaetos*)
Greater sandhill crane (*Grus candadensis tabida*)
Light-footed clapper rail (*Rallus longirostris levipes*)
Trumpeter swan (*Cygnus buccinator*)
White-tailed kite (*Elanus leucurus*)
Yuma clapper rail (*Rallus longirostris yumanensis*)

MAMMALS

Bighorn sheep (*Ovis canadensis*)
Guadalupe fur seal (*Arctocephalus townsendi*)

Morro Bay kangaroo rat (*Dipodomys heermanni morroensis*)
Northern elephant seal (*Mirounga angustirostris*)
Pacific right whale (*Balaena glacialis*)
Ring-tailed cat (*Bassariscus astutus*)
Salt-marsh harvest mouse
(*Reithrodontomys raviventris*)
Southern sea otter (*Enhydra lutris nereis*)
Wolverine (*Gulo gulo*)

wolverine

Note: there have been no changes to this list since 2003.

As of April 2006, the California Department of Fish and Game listed the following regarding species found within California or off the coast of the state:

- 47 species state-listed as endangered
- 32 species state-listed as threatened
- 84 species federally listed as endangered*
- 40 species federally listed as threatened**

*represents 21.1 percent of all U.S. listed endangered animals as of 1/4/06
**represents 30.2 percent of all U.S. listed threatened animals as of 1/4/06

Rats!

A small, desert-dwelling rodent, the kangaroo rat has strong hind legs and jumps like, well, a tiny kangaroo. They eat seeds and grasses, burrow deep into the sand to escape the desert heat, and are primarily nocturnal. The kidneys of kangaroo rats are about four times as efficient as a human's kidneys—which means they rarely drink water, even if it's available.

If any Morro Bay kangaroo rats still exist (none have been seen in some years), it is on one small privately owned lot near Los Osos. Sadly, the owners refuse to allow the Department of Fish and Game access to the land to look for signs of the animal or trap individuals for captive breeding. Having been listed since 1970, the status of the Morro Bay kangaroo rat is at present unknown.

An Endangered Species Success Story?

California condors are still endangered (although the state of California lists them as stable). But they are being brought back from the brink of extinction through aggressive captive-breeding programs at three facilities: the Los Angeles Zoo, San Diego Wild Animal Park, and World Center for Birds of Prey in Boise, Idaho. In 1987 biologists captured all remaining wild condors and began breeding them; by 1991 the program began releasing birds to the wild regularly. In 2003, the first bird fledged in the wild since 1981—cause for celebration. In March 2006, a pair were seen exhibiting nesting behavior in Big Sur—the first time in more than a hundred years that these magnificent birds have been observed nesting in Northern California.

california condor

Condors aren't (ahem) out of the woods yet. Unanticipated hazards such as golden eagles, power lines, and lead poisoning (from ingesting bullet fragments in large game) still kill birds every year. But the future looks hopeful for the California condor.

CALIFORNIA CONDOR FACTS

- It has the largest wingspan (over 9 ft.) of any North American bird.
- The head and neck are bare of feathers for hygienic reasons—after all, they eat carrion.
- Condors may live for more than 50 years, and they mate for life.
- If an egg is lost, the condor lays another, so biologists often take the first egg to rear in captivity, encouraging a second egg.
- Because of its large size, cattle ranchers who observed condors feeding on dead calves often thought the birds themselves had killed the animal. Although it is a fallacy, this belief led to their almost complete extermination in the West.
- In 1982, only 22 California condors were left alive.
- As of 2006, there are approximately 275 California condors.

I DIDN'T KNOW THAT ALMANAC CALIFORNIA EDITION 2007

GET INVOLVED

The California Department of Fish and Game lists several ways that Californians can get involved with wildlife preservation. They include:

Volunteer programs – the Department is looking for help in specific wildlife areas and reserves.

Project Wild Aquatic – available to any group of 10 or more, PWA is an award-winning K–12 conservation and environmental education program emphasizing aquatic wildlife. Programs are facilitated by volunteers.

Keep Me Wild campaign – make sure your garbage is secure, to prevent wildlife from feeding on it; download educational materials (www.dfg.ca.gov/keepmewild/about.html) and pass on to your friends and neighbors.

Outdoor California – the department's full-color magazine features outdoor adventures and the status of the state's amazing wildlife resources; you can donate subscriptions to schools too.

Be observant – report poachers and pollution by calling 1-888-DFG-CalTIP.

Be really observant – West Nile virus watch: report dead birds to public health agencies or call 1-877-968-2473.

Get licensed – buy a hunting or fishing license to use California's resources.

Get involved locally – participate in local conservation planning and zoning.

Join – join local conservation groups and go on field trips. It's fun too!

Vote – know the conservation issues and vote on them.

Our Nation's Symbol

Need More Information?
www.dfg.ca.go

Looking for bald eagles?

The best time to see bald eagles in California is from December to March, when migrating birds arrive from breeding habitats far north of here to winter. (The state does have a population of year-round bald eagles too.) Eagles can be found alone or in small groups almost anywhere in the state, near lakes and rivers—but the very best place to see them in numbers is in the Klamath Basin National Wildlife Refuges complex near the California-Oregon border. Tule Lake is of particular note.

WORLD TRAVELERS

Whales do it. Lots of birds do it too. And so do monarch butterflies—making an arduous round-trip migration covering thousands of miles. But unlike birds or whales, individual monarchs only make the round-trip once. It is their great-great-grandchildren that return the following year to the same winter roosts, often to the very same tree! It works like this:

1. The first generation makes a massive southward migration in the fall, arriving in mid-October at locations along the California coastline. They mate in January, and depart on their spring migration no later than March.

2. As the migration begins, the monarchs lay their eggs inland on milkweed plants in the Sierra Nevada foothills. There they die.

3. The second generation hatches after four days and the caterpillar feeds on the milkweed for two weeks before spinning a chrysalis, in which it remains for ten days to two weeks. Then new butterflies journey over the mountains northward.

4. This egg–caterpillar–chrysalis–butterfly sequence is repeated three times as the monarchs fan out and move northward into Canada, enjoying the summer months (and more importantly, the milkweed). Think of it as a relay race.

5. The fifth generation, the longest-lived, flies back to California, making journeys of a hundred miles a day. It does not reproduce until it leaves in the spring (see step 1).

There are two populations of monarchs: those that live east of the Rockies winter in Michoacán, Mexico, while those living west of that mountain range winter in California. How the butterflies manage to return to the same location over a gap of generations is still a matter of some speculation!

MONARCH HANG-OUTS

- Fremont: Ardenwood Historic Farm
- Santa Cruz, Natural Bridges State Beach
- Pacific Grove: Monarch Grove Sanctuary
- Big Sur: Andrew Molera State Park
- Morro Bay: Morro Bay State Park
- Pismo Beach: Pismo State Beach
- Ventura: Camino Real Park
- Malibu, Point Mugu State Park
- Long Beach, El Dorado Nature Center
- Encinitas, Monarch Butterfly House (450 Ocean View Avenue)
- San Diego, UCSD campus (La Jolla Shores Drive at Azul Street)

Pacific Grove benefits by one of those happy accidents of nature that gladden the heart, excite the imagination, and instruct the young. On a certain day in the shouting springtime great clouds of orangy Monarch butterflies, like twinkling aery fields of flowers, sail high in the air on a majestic pilgrimage across Monterey Bay and land in the outskirts of Pacific Grove in the pine woods.

—JOHN STEINBECK, *Sweet Thursday,* 1954

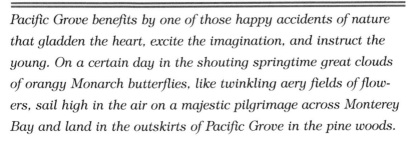

Butterfly Town U.S.A.

In addition to a late-October Butterfly Parade and other local celebrations, residents of Pacific Grove plant flowers that monarchs are partial to, such as lantana, yellow aster, and Mexican sage. And to make doubly sure the monarchs are made welcome, local ordinance 352 prohibits the molestation of monarchs; anyone caught in the act is liable to a $1,000 fine and/or jail time!

A Long Road Trip!

One of the oldest species on earth, gray whales have one of the longest migrations of any mammal—from summer feeding grounds in the Arctic to their winter location in the lagoons of Baja California, where they mate and give birth, the whales travel roughly 8,000 miles in each direction, one of the longest of any mammal. With California's 840 miles of coastline, that's plenty of whale-watching opportunities!

Gray whales pass California in late fall and early winter headed south, then return in late winter and early spring. The northward migration is of particular interest because the whales are traveling with newborn calves (and swimming against the current), so they are moving more slowly. They are also keeping the calves closer to shore. It is a spectacular sight.

Take one of the many coastal whale-watching expeditions if you want to be out on the water, but there are plenty of good sightings to be had from land, too, from coastal cliffs and headlands.

Thar' She Blows!

According to the Whale Watching Web ring, commercial whale watching dates from the winter of 1955 when Chuck Chamberlin offered trips out of San Diego to see gray whales as they passed on migration. The cost? One dollar! Marine biologist and pioneer whale-watcher Raymond M. Gilmore soon took over the trips. Gilmore headed whale research for the U.S. Fish and Wildlife Service, first in San Francisco and then in 1952 in San Diego at the Scripps Institution of Oceanography. The Gilmore trips, popular until his death in 1984, became something of a legend. Whale watching at its best, they were part science, part education, full of always unpredictable whale action, and lots of fun.

Gray Whale Facts

Male gray whales grow up to 45 feet long, while females are slightly larger.

Although some have reached weights of 30 to 40 tons, average weight is 16 tons (32,000 pounds).

Gestation period is about one year; females have calves every other year.

The white patches on a gray whale are areas where barnacles and lice have attached themselves.

Classified as a baleen whale, the gray's baleen—more like hair than teeth—act like a sieve to capture krill and other tiny crustaceans.

Gray whales surface every 3 to 5 minutes to breathe; they can remain submerged for up to 15 minutes.

Gray whales once existed in the Atlantic, but were hunted to extinction in the 1600s.

There are two Pacific Ocean populations: the Alaska-Baja population of 23,000, and a Japan-Korea population, which is close to extinction as it has fewer than 50 individuals.

California gray whales were removed from the endangered species list in 1994.

The brain size of whales is much larger than that of humans. Their cerebral cortexes are as convoluted. They are at least as social as humans. Anthropologists believe that the development of human intelligence has been critically dependent upon these three factors: brain volume, brain convolutions, and social interactions among individuals. Here we find a class of animals where the three conditions leading to human intelligence may be exceeded, and in some cases greatly exceeded.

—CARL SAGAN (1934–1996),
The Cosmic Connection, 1973

MYTH, MYSTERY, AND THE TRUTH

All we have to do is hear the opening notes of the soundtrack from *Jaws*, and, frankly, we'll drop our water bottles. While great whites are responsible for the majority of known attacks on humans, that doesn't mean you can believe everything you see and hear. Let's debunk some shark myths, and take a look at some of the amazing facts.

All sharks are the same
There are nearly 400 species of sharks, of all shapes, sizes, and habitat. Some are quite timid, while others are more curious.

The oceans are overrun with sharks
In fact, shark populations are declining worldwide, primarily due to bycatch, overfishing, and the fact that sharks mature relatively late and have few young.

Sharks have very little value
Au contraire! They are an important part of the ecosystem and play a critical role in the food chain.

Sharks are indiscriminant eating machines
Actually, although all are meat eaters, most sharks are pretty selective. It helps the digestion.

Shark species involved in unprovoked attacks in California waters from 1580 to 2005:

1.1%	Leopard
1.1%	Mako
2.2%	Blue
19.1%	Unknown
76.4%	White

Source: Florida Museum of Natural History (University of Florida)

Sharks eat all the time
Sharks eat periodically, depending on their metabolism and the availability of food in the area. Some sharks go for days or weeks between feeding.

Sharks will always attack humans
For the most part, they're just curious. And with more and more people invading shark habitats, the likelihood of a human-shark confrontation increases. Most attacks on humans are assumed to be accidental—a chance encounter. Furthermore, sharks generally spit humans out, because we're too bony.

Sharks have poor vision
Sharks can see color, and the lens in a shark's eye is up to seven times as powerful as a human's. They see contrast (light against dark) particularly well, and are attuned to shiny things, like fish scales (and jewelry).

Sharks aren't particularly smart

Recent studies indicate that many shark species exhibit playful behavior, possess problem-solving skills, and participate in social activities. In point of fact, the brain mass-to-body ratios of sharks are similar in size to those of mammals and other higher vertebrate species.

Shark cartilage pills can prevent or cure cancer

While sharks have demonstrated a strong resistance to cancer, they are not entirely immune to it, and there's absolutely no evidence that eating shark cartilage will help prevent or cure this disease in humans.

SHARK SAFETY

- Avoid swimming at dawn or dusk when your visibility is decreased and the shark's is increased.

- Surfers should keep a sharp eye: breaking waves make it difficult for sharks to see and determine whether you are prey.

- Do not wear jewelry in the water.

- Do not swim near schools of small fish or groups of sea lions, which are favorite foods of some sharks.

- Avoid water recreation activities near the mouths of rivers; this confluence, where fish enter the ocean and other animals congregate, attracts sharks.

- Don't swim alone, or get too far from shore. Refrain from excess splashing.

Humans are 250 times more likely to be killed by lightning than by a shark!

Yum Yum Yellow

Water safety gear is often made in bright yellow, because the color is readily seen by potential human rescuers. Problem is... sharks see it too. Some marine biologists refer to the color as yum yum yellow.

Save Our Sharks!

- When eating out or cooking in, choose sustainable seafood that is not fished in methods that produce bycatch. Don't patronize restaurants that serve this type of seafood.

- Don't eat shark fin soup at home or abroad; the fins are taken and the living shark is thrown back to die.

- Don't buy shark souvenirs.

- Don't buy "medicine" made of shark cartilage.

- Support conservation groups.

HaPPY DaiRY FaRMeRS

Agriculture (which includes fruit, vegetables, dairy, and wine) is the state's number-one industry, and the dairy industry is the state's number-one agricultural commodity. California has been the nation's leading dairy state since 1993—when it surpassed the previous leader, Wisconsin, in milk production. Here are some other interesting facts about California's dairy industry:

- California produces approximately 19 percent of the nation's milk supply.
- California's 2,200 dairy families house 1.5 million milk cows. Approximately one out of every six dairy cows in the U.S. lives in California.
- Dairy cows are milked 2 to 3 times a day and produce 6 to 7 gallons a day, over 2,000 gallons a year.
- California dairies produce 3.5 billion gallons of milk per year.
- California's dairy industry employs over 42,000 people.
- The average size of a dairy herd in California is 656 cows.
- There are six breeds of dairy cows in California: the black and white Holstein, the Jersey, the Brown Swiss, the Guernsey, the Ayrshire, and the Milking Shorthorn.
- Approximately 46 percent of all California milk goes to make cheese.
- If California were a separate nation, it would rank 8th in the world in cows milk production, 5th in the world in cheese production, and 9th in the world in butter production.

Source: USDA, California Dairy Farmers Association and California Dairy Herd Improvement Association

California's Top Dairy Counties

23.5%	Tulare
13.2%	Merced
10.5%	San Bernardino
10.3%	Stanislaus
8.1 %	Kings
7.3 %	Riverside
6.3 %	San Joaquin
5.4 %	Fresno
4.2 %	Kern
2.6 %	Madera
2.1 %	Sonoma
0.8 %	Humboldt

Source: Community Alliance for Responsible Environmental Stewardship

One of the most popular ad campaigns of the new century is the California Milk Advisory Board's award-winning "California's Happy Cows" commercials for Real California Cheese. Now with eighteen commercials featuring the sassy bovines since the first aired in late 2000 and consumer demand for T-shirts and stuffed toys still strong, the campaign shows no sign of slowing.

You Have Two Cows ...

Anarchism: You have two cows. Either you sell the milk at a fair price or your neighbors try to take the cows and kill you.

Communism (pure): You have two cows. Your neighbors help you take care of them, and you all share the milk.

Communism (Soviet): You have two cows. You have to take care of them, but the government takes all the milk.

Democracy: You have two cows. Your neighbors decide who gets the milk.

Dictatorship: You have two cows. The government takes both and shoots you.

Fascism: You have two cows. The government takes both, hires you to take care of them, and sells you the milk.

Feudalism: You have two cows. Your lord takes some of the milk.

Socialism: You have two cows. The government takes them and puts them in a barn with everyone else's cows, and gives you as much milk as you need.

Totalitarianism: You have two cows. The government takes them and denies they ever existed. Milk is banned.

California Cows Fail Emissions Test

That's right. Dairy cows in the San Joaquin Valley produce more smog-forming gases than cars, according to local air quality regulators. One dairy cow annually emits almost 20 pounds of smog-forming gases. The region's dairy industry currently includes some 2.5 million cattle. You do the math!

50,000,000 POUNDS OF GAS. WHEW!

CALIFORNIA'S INTERESTING ZOOS & AQUARIUMS

AQUARIUM OF THE PACIFIC

100 Aquarium Wy., Long Beach 90802 / (562) 590-3100

Opened in 1998, this visually stunning aquarium focuses on the Pacific Ocean with three permanent galleries, Southern California and Baja, Northern Pacific, and Tropical Pacific. It is one of the largest aquariums in the U.S.

BIRCH AQUARIUM

2300 Expedition Wy., La Jolla 92037 / (858) 534-34S74

The Scripps Institution of Oceanography has maintained an aquarium and museum dedicated to public education and enjoyment since 1903, pioneering the way we think about marine biology.

LOS ANGELES ZOO & BOTANICAL GARDENS

5333 Zoo Dr., Los Angeles 90027 / (323) 644-4200

With a proud history dating back to 1885, the Los Angeles Zoo is at the forefront of habitat and conservation efforts (particularly the California condor program). The zoo is also an accredited botanical garden.

The San Francisco Zoo's bald eagle hatchling Colbert (born April 17, 2006) was named after comedian Stephen Colbert of **The Daily Show;** *Colbert (the human) was also named one of* **Time** *magazine's* **100 Most Influential People of 2006.**

MONTEREY BAY AQUARIUM

886 Cannery Row, Monterey 93940 / (831) 648-4800

One of the largest and most respected aquariums in the world, the aquarium has two ground-breaking exhibits: the California coast

The San Francisco Zoo started when William Randolph Hearst bet one of his reporters that there were no grizzly bears left in California. Well, there were.

The Los Angeles Zoo was the first major zoo in the U.S. to bar visitors from feeding its animals.

The land for the Santa Ana Zoo was donated with the stipulation that there always be 50 monkeys in residence.

marine life, and the one-million-gallon tank that was the world's largest single-paned window when it was built (56 feet long and 17 feet high, it's actually five pieces of acrylic).

SAN DIEGO ZOO
2920 Zoo Dr., San Diego 92101 / (619) 231-1515

This world-renowned zoo is a pioneer of "cageless" exhibits, and is one of the world's few major zoos to be almost entirely open-air, including free-flight aviaries. It also operates the San Diego Wild Animal Park next door, which displays animals in an even freer condition. Maintaining a research division, the zoo's a world leader in conservation efforts, and is literally the last chance for some species.

The Giraffe With the "Broken" Neck

One of the most popular animals at the Santa Barbara Zoo is the giraffe with a neck deformity. This Baringo Giraffe was born normally in the San Diego Wild Animal Park in 1986, but as she grew she developed a bend in her neck. The deformity does not cause her pain and is likely caused by a benign bone tumor in one of her joints.

From Birds to Big Cats

Actress Tippi Hedren may be best known for her work in Alfred Hitchcock's *The Birds*, but it's her work with big cats that gives her the most satisfaction. Hedren met her first lion on a movie set in 1969 and fell in love, but it was producing her film *Roar* that led directly to the establishment of the Shambala Preserve, a nonprofit wildlife rescue sanctuary in the high desert near Acton (north of Los Angeles) in 1972. Shambala provides a home for exotic animals, most of whom were born in captivity, from circuses, zoos, and private individuals; often they've been abused or abandoned. (In June 2006 the preserve took in two tigers from Michael Jackson's Neverland Ranch; like other residents, the animals arrived with no endowment for their future care.) The Shambala Preserve does not breed, buy, sell, or trade animals, although tours are given once a month, often by Tippi herself, to help raise the minimum $75,000 needed to run the preserve each month. Currently there are nearly seventy residents of Shambala, including African lions, Siberian and Bengal tigers, leopards, servals, mountain lions, bobcats, a lynx, a Florida panther, a snow leopard, a cheetah, and elephant ... and one Tippi Hedren!

Shambala Preserve / 6867 Soledad Canyon, Acton 93510 / (661) 268-0380

Guardian Angel

On Thanksgiving Day 2003, nine-year-old Angel Arellano wrote a letter to the *Fresno Bee.* Worried because she'd heard that the zoo was experiencing financial problems, she wrote that if everyone in Fresno gave a dollar to the zoo, she believed it might be saved. And she enclosed a dollar.

Her sincere letter caught the attention of the folks at the paper, and the resulting publicity touched a chord with Fresno residents and former residents, inspiring thousands of individuals to send donations. To date, donations ranging from a dollar to $10,000 total $236,000, and have come from as far away as Great Britain.

Angel's efforts have earned her accolades, too, and she was mentioned in the Congressional Record on February 3, 2004, by California Sen. Barbara Boxer.

Want to help? Send contributions to Dollars From Angels, Fresno Chaffee Zoo Maintenance Fund, 894 W. Belmont Ave., Fresno, CA 93728.

Wildlife WayStation

Internationally recognized for its ongoing, charitable efforts to rescue, rehabilitate, and relocate wild and exotic animals, Wildlife WayStation has saved the lives of 76,000 animals. Abused, injured, ill, abandoned, and orphaned animals come to this 24-hour-a-day operation from all over the world. Many are placed in reputable zoos or animal parks. Four hundred currently reside here permanently, including bears, lions, tigers, wolves, eagles, and alligators, looked after by a small permanent staff and more than 300 volunteers. Wildlife WayStation is supported solely through donations and fundraising, and receives no government funds.

14831 Little Tujunga Canyon Rd., Angeles National Forest 91342 / (818) 899-5201

NO SHRINKING VIOLET

The yellow-billed magpie is the only bird found exclusively in California, although it is closely related to the black-billed version east of the Sierra Nevada. Along with its cousins, crows and jays, this large, iridescent black and white bird is extremely gregarious—and pretty noisy! Given that they live and move around in colonies, which gives rise to endless disputes and minor feuds, magpies are a

lot of fun to watch. But watch out! They've been observed aggressively mobbing predators or other perceived threats—including humans.

Found mostly in the Central Valley and its foothills, as well as in pockets along the coastal ranges, the magpie requires large trees for nesting and open ranges for foraging on the ground, where they mainly eat insects, especially grasshoppers, but also carrion, earthworms, acorns, and fruit in fall and winter.

Magpies build huge domed nests (about three feet across) of loosely piled sticks and mud. Look for these nests in winter, thirty to eighty feet off the ground in sycamore, cottonwood, and oak trees.

Looking for Magpies?

The California Department of Fish and Game recommends the following as good locations for magpie watching:

Battle Creek Wildlife Area

Gray Lodge Wildlife Area

Effie Yeaw Nature Center/American River Parkway

Folsom Lake State Recreation Area

Caswell Memorial State Park

Los Banos Wildlife Area/Valley Grasslands

Joseph Grant County Park

Lake San Antonio

Santa Margarita Lake

WATCHABLE WILDLIFE

Here are a few general tips for observing California wildlife...

- Keep your distance, at least 100 yards. Use binoculars to get close.
- On the water, keep boats speeds slow. If approached, put the engine in neutral and allow the animal to pass.
- Be quiet. Seal pups have been trampled by adult seals that were frightened by tourists.
- Don't stay long; half an hour is enough.
- Stay clear of mothers with young.
- Don't try to "save" animals. Get professional help.
- In particular, don't rescue "orphans." Mom is usually close by.
- Never surround an animal. It should have an escape route.
- Leave pets at home (best) or keep them leashed.
- Don't litter. Better yet, carry a trash bag with you to pick up litter you might see.
- Don't feed wild animals.

The Farallon Islands

Unless you're a marine biologist or work for the U.S. Fish & Wildlife Service, it's unlikely that you'll get close to the rocky Farallon Islands, located twenty-eight miles west of the Golden Gate Bridge. But they're very, very special.

You see, the Farallons contain the largest seabird nesting colony south of Alaska. Over 200,000 seabirds frequent the island chain, and twelve species breed here. This refuge holds the largest colony of western gulls in the world. It supports half the world's population of Ashy storm-petrels. And that's just the birds. The threatened Steller sea lion and endangered green and leatherback turtles—as well as hundreds of other species—pass by or stop here.

But in order to protect these and other animals from over a century of abuse, access to the islands is strictly limited, including boating. During breeding season (between March 15 and August 15), vessel traffic is prohibited within 300 feet.

So... stay away! We're just thankful that someone (it was Teddy Roosevelt who established this National Wildlife Refuge in 1909) is looking out for the Farallons ... for the sake of our children's children.

BIRDING FROM NORTH TO SOUTH

We couldn't possibly give you the lowdown on every great birding venue in California—after all, the Golden State is a natural paradise teeming with wildlife.

HUMBOLDT BAY NATIONAL WILLIFE REFUGE

1020 Ranch Rd., Loleta 95551 / (707) 733-5406

Just outside historic Eureka on the dramatic, jagged northwestern coast, the Humboldt Bay NWR encloses a vast wetlands that is a resting spot for migratory birds, including tens of thousands of shorebirds, ducks, geese, swans, and black brant. In fact, on a typical winter day, it's not unusual for over a hundred thousand birds to use the bay—a spectacular sight that alone makes the trip north worthwhile. Peak viewing season for most species is September through March.

While you're in the area, be sure to visit the Humboldt Botanical Garden, Redwood National Park, and Humboldt Redwoods State Park.

HAVASU NATIONAL WILDLIFE REFUGE

317 Mesquite Ave., Needles 92363 / (760) 326-3853

Located along thirty beautiful miles of the Colorado River as it flows through the Mojave Desert, this refuge is one of the last natural stretches of the river. The topography includes desert sand dunes, a large marsh, and backwater areas, as well as the spectacular Topock Gorge and mountainous terrain that supports the elusive desert bighorn sheep.

While you're in the area, you might enjoy driving historic Route 66, which passes through Needles; if you enjoy roadside attractions, be sure to see the original London Bridge (yes, that London Bridge!) in Lake Havasu City. It's Arizona's second largest tourist attraction...after the Grand Canyon.

BEAR IN MIND

There are over 20,000 black bears in California, which means that if you enjoy hiking or camping in wilderness areas, the chance of encountering one is pretty high. Possessed of a keen sense of smell, these smart, strong creatures know what an ice chest looks like, and they can break car windows and rip open trunks. Here's what to do if you visit bear country:

Prevention is key:
1. Do not leave food or any item with a smell (such as sunscreen) in your car.
2. Take out infant and child seats (they smell like food).
3. Store everything in a bear-proof container (available at many parks).
4. Place garbage in the park's bear-proof dumpsters.
5. When hiking, make noise to let bears know you're there.
6. Never, ever intentionally feed a bear.

In case of encounters:
1. Do not approach a bear—especially a cub. Give it plenty of room to pass.
2. Act as if you are a threat: make lots of noise, raise your arms (for height), open your jacket (for size).
3. Stand together with other people to look intimidating; pick up small children.
4. Throw small sticks and stones to scare it away.
5. Do not run from a bear; instead, make eye contact without staring.
6. If attacked, fight back.
7. Report all bear encounters to a ranger right away.

36 Million People Can't Be Wrong

It's been an exciting 156 years. From a barely populated western frontier situated on a lot of desert, California is now the world's eighth largest economy, based on a complex and diverse set of industries. But an economy isn't built without people, and California's economic history is one of historic population booms.

BOOM!

When gold was discovered in 1848 on the American River near Sutter's Mill, the first boom was on. Within two years, more than 200,000 people had made their way to the state to look for gold. The real profits were made by the ship owners and merchants who brought and sold suppliers to the miners. In one year, the population of San Francisco went from 800 to 50,000. By 1860, the population of the state had risen from the 1848 level of 26,000 to 380,000.

BOOM!

From 1928 to 1935 a drought in the southern plains states preceded by years of bad farming techniques produced what we call the Dust Bowl. Thousands of farms were foreclosed on and more than 500,000 people became homeless. Drawn to the hope of California, over a million migrants arrived in the state by 1945.

California's population in 2005: 36,132,147

BOOM!

An industrial boom—aerospace, shipbuilding, and technology—spurred by World War II, combined with a drain on the workforce as over 700,000 Californians joined the armed forces, caused the next migration. Over 1.9 million people arrived in the state between 1940 and 1945.

BOOM!

After WWII, California's population continued to boom, at a rate of half a million per year for the next twenty-five years, fueled by federal defense spending on the Cold War. Infrastructure and housing needs kept the population busy and the economy booming right along with the population. In 1963, California overtook New York as the nation's most populous state. By 1970, the state's population was at 20 million ... and now it's more than 36 million!

THE FIRST PYRAMID SCHEME?

Silk has always been a bit of an exotic commodity. Made from the protein fiber obtained from the cocoon of silkworm larvae, silk has long been prized for its shimmering beauty, making it highly valuable. And some folks are always on the lookout for easy money.

This was the case in the mid-1860s, when a Frenchman by the name of Louis Prevost began raising silkworms near San Jose ... not to make silk, necessarily, but to produce lots and lots of eggs, which would then be sold to European silk producers. He was quite a promoter, and his idea got the attention of someone at the California State Agricultural Society.

By 1867, the state was in on the act, promising a $250 bonus to anyone who planted mulberry trees (silkworm food). Mulberry planting proliferated at an alarming rate, and the state's treasury was threatened with bankruptcy as people sold silkworm eggs to each other. But as would-be silk farmers discovered that the silkworms were high-maintenance little devils, what began as a craze collapsed overnight, as interest crawled away.

China is still the largest producer of silk in the world. But there are still lots and lots of mulberry trees in California.

I spent two hours in questioning Mr. Prevost about the silk culture—and crowding him down to categorical answers without permitting him to wander off into other departments of the subject—and what I don't know about this business now is hardly worth knowing.

—MARK TWAIN (1835–1910),
San Francisco Bulletin, December 7, 1866

SiLiCON

SIL·I·CON, (SI-LI-KN, SI-L-KÄN), NOUN

From New Latin silica + English -on (as in carbon), 1817 : a tetravalent nonmetallic element that occurs combined as the most abundant element next to oxygen in the earth's crust and is used especially in ferrosilicon for steelmaking, in other alloys, and in semiconductors.

O Pioneers!

They arrived after the age of covered wagons, but Lee de Forest, Fred Terman, and William Shockley all played a part in setting the stage for the industry that would come to be Silicon Valley.

Arriving in California in 1910 with a PhD from Yale University, **Lee de Forest** brought with him his own invention, the Audion vacuum tube, which allowed for amplification of wireless signals. He went on to work for the Federal Telegraph Company in Palo Alto, one of the first electronics companies in the area, where he continued to take an interest in wireless technology. The work that de Forest and his colleagues did at FTC can arguably be considered the birth of the electronics industry; it opened the door for the development of radio, television, radar ... and, ultimately, computers.

Often called the "Father of Silicon Valley," professor **Fred Terman** taught electrical engineering at Stanford University. As Stanford's provost, Terman expanded the science, statistics, and engineering departments and pursued research grants from the Department of Defense. Patents and grants made Stanford a world-class research university. Two of his PhD students were William Hewlett and David Packard, who went on to form one of Silicon Valley's first companies, the electronics giant Hewlett-Packard Company.

Finally, physicist **William Shockley**—who helped invent the transistor and won the 1956 Nobel Prize for it, along with his co-inventors—founded Shockley Transistor Corporation in Mountain View in the 1950s to work on semiconductors. A list of his early employees is a Who's Who of the future of the high tech industry. Silicon Valley is often considered to be a direct result of his work done here and at Stanford University.

Beautiful Downtown Silicon Valley

Yes, Virginia, it really is a place. Well, sort of. When first used, the phrase really just referred to the large number of silicon chip companies in the South Bay area, but it's come to mean the region itself. Stretching from as far north as Redwood City, west to Los Gatos and Saratgoa, and pulling up short in San Jose, Silicon Valley is a place, an industry, and, some say, a state of mind.

Silicon Valley has more millionaires per capita than anywhere else in the United States.

"SILICON VALLEY USA"

Journalist Don Hoefler was the first to use the phrase in print, to describe "the congeries of electronics firms mushrooming in Santa Clara County." He was writing a series of articles for the weekly trade newspaper *Electronic News*, titled "Silicon Valley USA," the first appeared on January 11, 1971. Speaking in a phone interview almost fourteen years later to the day, Hoefler allowed that he'd heard "easterners" use the term; however, Hoefler is widely credited with placing the concept into the popular imagination.

Apple: A Big Byte

Long before PC was a term to describe behavior, and even before it meant a computer running on technology invented in, well, a state to the north of California, PC was short for "personal computer." And the first personal computer company was Apple, founded as a partnership on April 1, 1976. The Apple I, sold mostly to hobbyists that same year, was the first to combine a keyboard with a micro-

An Apple ll with two external hard drives.

processor and a connection to a monitor. By 1977, Apple had developed and was selling the Apple II. It looked like an appliance—not a piece of electronic wizardry—and it revolutionized the industry. Perhaps we should say it created the industry, although there were others making computers at the time (and soon would be many more!). But the Apple II was the first computer many folks had seen. It was affordable for middle-class families. It was, we'll say it—a personal computer. (Actually the Apple II was called a "home computer." The IBM PC, which popularized the acronym, came along in August 1981.)

WHO'S WHO IN SILICON VALLEY

While there are thousands of high technology companies headquartered in Silicon Valley, these are listed in the Forbes 500 (date founded in parentheses):

- Adobe Systems (1982)
- Advanced Micro Devices (1969)
- Agilent Technologies (1999)*
- AKANOC Solutions Group Inc. (2004)
- Altera (1983)
- Apple Computer (1976)
- Applied Materials (1967)
- BEA Systems (1995)
- Cadence Design Systems (1988)
- Cisco Systems (1984)
- Corsair Memory (1994)
- DreamWorks Animation (1994)
- eBay (1995)
- Electronic Arts (1982)
- Google (1998)
- Hewlett-Packard (1939)
- Intel (1968)
- Intuit (1983)
- Juniper Networks (1996)
- Logitech (1981)
- Maxtor (1982)
- National Semiconductor (1959)
- Network Appliance (1992)
- NVIDIA Corporation (1993)
- Oracle Corporation (1977)
- Siebel Systems (1993)
- SPOCK Networks (2005)
- Sun Microsystems (1982)
- Symantec (1982)
- Synopsys (1986)
- Varian Medical Systems (1985)
- Xilinx (1984)
- Yahoo! (1995)

*Actually a part of Hewlett-Packard's original 1939 operation, Agilent was spun off in 1999.

I DIDN'T KNOW THAT ALMANAC CALIFORNIA EDITION 2007

Have You Ever Googled Yourself?

Unless you've been visiting Mars for the last few years, you know that Google started as an Internet search engine, using technology that Larry Page and Sergey Brin developed. Ten years ago, Page and Brin were computer science PhD students at Stanford University. Today, they're billionaires (though neither has a PhD). In between, there is Google. Here are a few things you may not know:

- Google is translated into 97 languages.

- It maintains a presence in over 88 countries, including China.

- At 200 *million* requests a day, Google is the world's largest and most active search engine.

The welcome sign to the Googleplex.

- Google's first data center was in Page's dorm room.

- The ratio of male to female employees at Google is roughly 70/30.

- Google was incorporated on September 7, 1998, at a friend's garage in Menlo Park.

- The company was granted U.S. Patent 6,285,999 for its PageRank ranking mechanism on September 4, 2001.

- Google was added to the S&P 500 index on March 31, 2006.

- Brin and Page each accept a base salary of $1.00.

The verb, "to google," was officially added to both the Merriam Webster Collegiate Dictionary and the Oxford English Dictionary in July, 2006, as a verb meaning "to use the Google search engine to obtain information on the Internet"!

- All Google employees are allowed to spend 20 percent of their company time working on a project of personal interest.

- Company headquarters, in Mountain View, is the Googleplex.

- Google has turned a profit every year since 2001.

- Google's initial public offering in August, 2004, raised $1.67 billion, making many employees paper millionaires.

- Page and Brin are still enrolled in the Stanford doctoral program, although they are "on leave."

An Online Yard Sale

Quick—can you remember the first time you heard of eBay? It may have been during that Beanie Babies collecting craze in the late '90s, fueled, in part, by the fledgling auction site. Or maybe it was the day a ten-year-old grilled cheese sandwich sold for $28,000 (it had a likeness of the Virgin Mary toasted into it, or so they say). Since its inception on September 4, 1995, this online auction site has been bringing buyers and sellers together. A rundown of unusual items sold on eBay would require an entire book, but here are some eBay points of interest:

- First sale: creator Pierre Omidyar's broken laser pointer (for $13.93)
- Number of registered eBay members in 2006: 100 million
- Top three most popular categories: collectables; clothing, shoes, and accessories; and entertainment (mostly music)
- Most expensive item sold: in 2006, $85 million for a 405-foot yacht
- Percentage of items that receive no bids: 54
- Time of day most items sell: mid-evening (people surfing after dinner)
- Elvis is in the building: water from a cup Elvis drank from at a 1977 concert (kept by a then–13-year-old fan) was auctioned for $455

The Best California Companies to Work For

COMPANY	LOCATION	EMPLOYEES
Amgen	Thousand Oaks	11,374
Autodesk	San Rafael	2,098
Cisco Systems	San Jose	26,644
Genentech	So. San Francisco	8,121
Granite Construction	Watsonville	4,300
Hot Topic	City of Industry	8,314
Intel	Santa Clara	48,655
Intuit	Mountain View	6,516
Men's Wearhouse	Houston	10,757
Morrison & Foerster	San Francisco	2,145
Network Appliance	Sunnyvale	2,712
Nugget Markets	Woodland	1,091
Qualcomm	San Diego	7,562
Standard Pacific	Irvine	2,317
Vision Service Plan	Rancho Cordova	1,915
Yahoo	Sunnyvale	5,444

Source: *Fortune*, "100 Best Companies to Work For 2006"

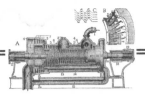

MULTITASKING

Do you know what steam cogeneration is? Neither did we ... but here it is. The California oilfields produce "heavy" oil (oil too thick to flow on its own), so in order to get it out, steam is pumped in to warm it up and make it behave a little less like molasses in January. Cogeneration simply means that before the steam used in the oil well, it's put through turbines—which produce massive amounts of electricity! Now that's what we call multitasking!

INDUSTRY	WHY
Pharmaceuticals	Very generous benefits
Software	Casual atmosphere
Communications equipment	Employee access to CEO
Biotechnology	Workers are shareholders
Engineering, construction	Corporate charitable donations decided by employees
Clothing retailer	No dress code
Semiconductors	Employees speak their minds
Software	Legendary parties
Clothing retailer	Promotion from within
Legal services	Generous salaries
Net hardware	Employee appreciation
Grocer	Very generous benefits
Communications equipment	Stock, education for employees
Homebuilders	Discounts on homes
Health care	Employee appreciation
Internet	Perks and stock options

The 20 Largest Privately Owned California Companies

NAME	REVENUE (IN BILLIONS)	INDUSTRY	EMPLOYEES
Bechtel	17.38	Technical consulting	40,000
Platinum Equity	8.00	Multicompany	45,000
Capital Group Companies	7.77	Financial services	6,000
SAIC	7.19	Aerospace and defense	42,400
Murdock Holding Co.	6.25	Food processing	67,000
Levi Strauss & Co.	4.07	Apparel and textiles	8,850
Mervyns	3.40	Retail/discount	23,000
Raley's	3.30	Supermarkets	16,500
Stater Bros. Markets	3.25	Supermarkets	16,500
J.F. Shea Co., Inc.	3.08	Building: homes/ commercial	2,668
Consolidated Electric	2.60	Electrical equipment	5,200
Aecomm	2.50	Technical consulting	22,000
Kingston Technology	2.50	Computer peripherals	2,400
Save Mart Supermarkets	2.50	Supermarkets	10,500
E&J Gallo Winery	2.40	Beverages and tobacco	4,400
Fry's Electronics	2.25	Specialty retail	6,500
Golden State Foods	2.20	Food processing	2,500
Parsons	1.99	Technical consulting	10,000
Swinerton Inc.	1.84	Commercial building	1,450
Metro-Goldwyn-Mayer	1.73	Entertainment	500

Source: Forbes, "America's Largest Private Companies," November 2005.

As of 2005, California's economy was larger than all but seven national economies in the world.

TOP TWENTY RICHEST CALIFORNIANS

WHO	SOURCE	NET WORTH (IN MILLIONS)	RESIDES
Larry Ellison	Oracle	$17,000	Silicon Valley
Sergey Brin	Google	$11,000	San Francisco
Larry Page	Google	$11,000	San Francisco
Kirk Kerkorian	Investments, casinos	$10,000	Los Angeles
Sumner Redstone	Viacom	$8,400	Beverly Hills
Eli Broad	Investments	$5,500	Los Angeles
Gordon E. Moore	Intel	$4,600	Woodside
David Geffen	DreamWorks	$4,500	Malibu
Barbara Davis & family	Inheritance, oil	$4,000	Beverly Hills
David Howard Murdock	Investments	$4,000	Los Angeles
Eric Schmidt	Google	$4,000	Atherton
Charles R. Schwab	Discount stock brokerage	$3,800	Atherton
Charles B. Johnson	Franklin Resources	$3,700	San Mateo
George Lucas	Star Wars	$3,500	Marin County
Steve Jobs	Apple Computer, Pixar	$3,300	Palo Alto
Bradley Hughes	Public Storage	$3,200	Malibu
Rupert Johnson Jr.	Franklin Resources	$3,100	San Mateo
Roland Arnall	Mortgage banking	$3,000	Holmby Hills
David Filo	Yahoo	$3,000	Mountain View
Haim Saban	Television	$2,800	Beverly Hills

Source: *Forbes* magazine, "The 400 Richest Americans," September 2005.

#21?

Just missed out list:
Steven Spielberg, $2,700, Movies, Pacific Palisades.
You knew he had to be there!

There are more Californians on the Forbes list than from any other state.

DAY / YEAR	DAY / WEEK	DAY / MONTH	SUN RISE	SUN SET	LENGTH OF DAY	TIDE AM	TIDE PM	MOON	ON THIS DAY
1	Mon	1	7:25	5:02	9/37	3:13L 9:41H	4:53 L	○	1855: Sacramento officially becomes the state's capital.
2	Tues	2	7:25	5:02	9/37	12:0 H 4:11L 10:31H	5:39 L	○	1961: The Great Rose Bowl Hoax, Caltech pranksters change the Huskies fans flip cards to read "Caltech."
3	Wed	3	7:25	5:03	9/38	12:03H 5:04L 11:18H	6:22L	○	1977: Apple Computer is incorporated by Steve Jobs and Steve Wozniak in Cupertino.
4	Thurs	4	7:26	5:04	9/38	1:31H 5:53L	12:02H 7:02L	○	1936: A short animated film called *Mickey's Polo Team*, is released by Disney.
5	Fri	5	7:26	5:05	9/39	2:10H 6:41L	12:45H 7:39L	○	1933: Construction of the Golden Gate Bridge begins.
6	Sat	6	7:26	5:06	9/40	2:47H 7:28L	1:26H 8:15L	○	1860: The steamer *Northerner* sinks off Cape Mendocino killing 38.
7	Sun	7	7:26	5:07	9/41	3:22H 8:17L	2:08H 8:49L	☽	1781: The Spanish establish a pueblo on the Colorado River.
8	Mon	8	7:25	5:08	9/43	3:55H 9:09L	2:53H 9:23L	☽	1863: Construction of the Central Pacific Railroad begins.
9	Tues	9	7:25	5:09	9/44	4:28H 10:06L	3:46H 9:57L	☽	1847: *The California Star* publishes its first issue.
10	Wed	10	7:25	5:10	9/45	5:01H 11:08L	4:52H 10:33L	☽	1913: Richard M. Nixon is born.
11	Thurs	11	7:25	5:11	9/46	5:37H	12:13L 6:18H 11:15L	◑	1880: A total solar eclipse of the sun occurs in San Francisco.
12	Fri	12	7:25	5:12	9/47	6:15H	1:18L 7:58H	●	1876: Author Jack London is born in San Francisco
13	Sat	13	7:25	5:13	9/48	12:04L 6:59H	2:17L 9:26H	●	1847: The "Capitulation of Cahuenga" ends resistance to American rule.
14	Sun	14	7:24	5:14	9/50	1:02L 7:46H	3:10L 10:31H	●	1951: First NFL pro bowl game held in Los Angeles.
15	Mon	15	7:24	5:15	9/51	2:04L 8:35H	3:58L 11:20H	●	1974: The TV show *Happy Days* premieres on ABC.
16	Tues	16	7:24	5:16	9/52	3:03L 9:23H	4:41L	☾	1847: John C. Frémont appointed military govenor of California.

Every man should be born again on the first day of January. Start with a fresh page. Take up one hole more in the buckle if necessary, or let down one, according to circumstances; but on the first of January let every man gird himself once more, with his face to the front, and take no interest in the things that were and are past.

—HENRY WARD BEECHER (1813–1887)

DAY / YEAR	DAY / WEEK	DAY / MONTH	SUN RISE	SUN SET	LENGTH OF DAY	TIDE AM	TIDE PM	MOON	ON THIS DAY
17	Wed	17	7:23	5:17	9/54	12:00H 3:55L 10:09H	5:22L	●	1944: The Northridge Earthquake strikes in Los Angeles.
18	Thurs	18	7:23	5:18	9/55	12:35H 4:45L 10:55H	6:01L	●	1935: The San Francisco Museum of Art opens it doors on the 4th floor of the War Memorial Veterans Bldg.
19	Fri	19	7:22	5:19	9/57	1:09H 5:32L 11:40H	6:40L	●	1889: Alexis Godey, a California frontiersman, dies.
20	Sat	20	7:22	5:20	9/58	1:41H 6:21L	12:26H 7:17L	●	1937: Coldest temperature in state, -45, in Boca.
21	Sun	21	7:21	5:21	10/00	2:14H 7:12L	1:14H 7:55L	●	1985: Ronald Reagan is inaugurated for his second term as President.
22	Mon	22	7:21	5:22	10/01	2:48H 8:08L	2:06H 8:33L	●	1849: *The Alta California* becomes first daily paper in California.
23	Tues	23	7:20	5:23	10/03	3:24H 9:07L	3:03H 9:12L	●	1960: *USS Trieste* breaks depth record.
24	Wed	24	7:20	5:24	10/04	4:03H 10:12L	4:11H 9:53L	●	1848: Gold is discovered in California.
25	Thurs	25	7:19	5:25	10/06	4:45H 11:22L	5:35H 10:39L	◑	1971: Charles Manson and 3 others found guilty of murder.
26	Fri	26	7:18	5:27	10/09	5:34H 11:08L	12:36L 10:33L	◐	2005: Three trains crash in Glendale, killing 11 and injuring 200.
27	Sat	27	7:18	5:28	10/10	6:30H	1:49L 8:56H	◐	1894: California Midwinter Expo opens in Golden Gate Park.
28	Sun	28	7:17	5:29	10/12	12:42L 7:31H	2:55H 10:12H	◐	1986: Space Shuttle Challenger explodes, killing all 7 aboard.
29	Mon	29	7:16	5:30	10/14	1:58L 6:59H	3:53H 9:26L	◐	1995: 49ers defeat Chargers in Super Bowl XXIX.
30	Tues	30	7:16	5:31	10/15	3:09L 8:34H	4:42H 11:08L	◐	1847: Yerba Buena is renamed San Francisco.
31	Wed	31	7:15	5:32	10/17	4:10L	5:26L	○	1848: Lt. Col. Frémont found guilty of treason.

● NEW MOON　◐ FIRST QUARTER　○ FULL MOON　◐ LAST QUARTER

DAY / YEAR	DAY / WEEK	DAY / MONTH	SUN RISE	SUN SET	LENGTH OF DAY	TIDE AM	TIDE PM	MOON	ON THIS DAY
32	Thurs	1	7:14	5:33	10/19	12:32H 5:01L 11:14H	6:04L	○	1827: Jedediah Strong Smith is first American to reach Mexican California overland.
33	Fri	2	7:13	5:34	10/21	1:05H 5:48L 11:56H	6:39L	○	1848: Treaty of Guadalupe Hidalgo formally ends the Mexican War and California is ceded to the U.S.
34	Sat	3	7:12	5:35	10/23	1:35H 6:30L	12:36H 7:10L	○	1857: The first issue of the *Sacramento Bee* is published.
35	Sun	4	7:11	5:37	10/26	2:03H 7:12L	1:14H 7:40L	☽	1974: Patty Hearst is kidnapped.
36	Mon	5	7:10	5:38	10/28	2:29H 7:53L	1:53H 8:08L	☽	1919: United Artists is incorporated.
37	Tues	6	7:09	5:39	10/30	2:54H 8:36L	2:35H 8:36L	☽	1985: Steve Wozniak leaves Apple Computer.
38	Wed	7	7:08	5:40	10/32	3:19H 9:23L	3:23H 9:05L	☽	1914: Charlie Chaplin's first film, *Kid AutoRaces at Venice,* is released.
39	Thurs	8	7:07	5:41	10/34	3:47H 10:15L	4:21H 9:37L	☽	1984: Pipe bomb explodes at L.A. Summer Olympics, killing two.
40	Fri	9	7:06	5:42	10/36	4:19H 11:14L	5:40H 10:14L	☽	1960: 1st Hollywood Walk of Fame star awarded to Joanne Woodward.
41	Sat	10	7:05	5:43	10/38	5:00H	12:21L 7:26H 11:02L	◐	1950: Olympic Gold Medalist Mark Spitz born in Modesto.
42	Sun	11	7:04	5:44	10/40	5:51H	1:30L 9:06H	◖	1973: Vietnam releases the first American prisoners of war.
43	Mon	12	7:03	5:45	10/42	21:11L 6:54H	2:33L 10:10H	◖	2004: San Francisco begins issuing marriage licenses to same-sex couples.
44	Tues	13	7:02	5:47	10/45	1:30L 7:59H	3:27L 10:52H	◖	2000: Last original "Peanuts" comic strip appears in newspapers.
45	Wed	14	7:01	5:48	10/47	2:41L 8:59H	4:14L 11:27H	◖	1886: 1st trainload of oranges exported via the transcontinental railroad.
46	Thurs	15	7:00	5:49	10/49	3:40L 9:54H	4:55L 11:58H	☾	2004: John Daly wins 1st PGA Tour event in 9 years in San Diego.

Loud are the thunder drums in the tents of the mountains.
Oh, long, long have we eaten chia seeds
and dried deer's flesh of the summer killing.
We are tired of our huts
and the smoky smell of our clothing.
We are sick with the desire for the sun
And the grass on the mountain.

—PAIUTE LATE WINTER SONG

DAY / YEAR	DAY / WEEK	DAY / MONTH	SUN RISE	SUN SET	LENGTH OF DAY	TIDE AM	TIDE PM	MOON	ON THIS DAY
47	Fri	16	6:58	5:50	10/52	4:33L 10:44H	5:34L	●	1867: Battle of Chimney Rock.
48	Sat	17	6:57	5:51	10/54	12:28H 5:23L 11:34H	6:11L	●	1972: Sales of Volkswagen Beetle exceeds sales for Ford Model-T.
49	Sun	18	6:56	5:52	10/56	12:58H 6:13L	12:23H 6:48L	●	1960: Opening ceremonies of Winter Olympics held in Squaw Valley.
50	Mon	19	6:55	5:53	10/58	1:29H 7:03L	1:14H 7:24L	●	1942: Internment of Japanese in camps throughout California.
51	Tues	20	6:54	5:54	11/00	2:02H 7:55L	2:08H 8:01L	●	1873: Univ. of California opens its first medical school.
52	Wed	21	6:52	5:55	11/03	2:37H 8:51L	3:08H 8:40L	●	1874: Oakland *Daily Tribune* publishes its first newspaper.
53	Thurs	22	6:51	5:56	11/05	3:16H 9:51L	4:17H 9:12L	◐	1856: 22-mile Sacramento Valley Railroad completed.
54	Fri	23	6:50	5:57	11/07	4:00H 10:57L	5:41H 10:10L	◑	1974: $4 million ransom demanded for release of Patty Hearst.
55	Sat	24	6:48	5:58	11/10	4:53H	12:11H 7:21H 11:13L	◐	1947: Actor and social activist Edward James Olmos born in East L.A.
56	Sun	25	6:47	5:59	11/12	5:58H	1:27L 8:53H	◑	1913: 16th Amendment to the Constitution is ratified: income tax.
57	Mon	26	6:46	6:00	11/14	12:35L 7:13H	2:36L 9:58H	◑	1863: President Lincoln signs the National Currency Act into law.
58	Tues	27	6:44	6:01	11/17	2:01L 8:26H	3:34L 10:46H	◑	1974: 1st issue of *People* magazine hits the stands.
59	Wed	28	6:43	6:02	11/19	3:13L	4:22L	◑	1849: Regular steamboat travel to California is commenced.

● NEW MOON   ◐ FIRST QUARTER   ○ FULL MOON   ◑ LAST QUARTER

DAY / YEAR	DAY / WEEK	DAY / MONTH	SUN RISE	SUN SET	LENGTH OF DAY	TIDE AM	TIDE PM	MOON	ON THIS DAY
60	Thurs	1	6:42	6:03	11/21	4:10L 10:22H	5:02L 11:56H	☾	1971: A bomb explodes in a men's room in the U.S. Capitol Building.
61	Fri	2	6:40	6:04	11/24	4:57L 11:08H	5:36L	○	2004: John Kerry wins the Super Tuesday primary in California.
62	Sat	3	6:39	6:05	11/26	12:25H 5:38L 11:50H	6:06L	○	1991: Rodney King is beaten and arrested by the LAPD.
63	Sun	4	6:37	6:06	11/29	12:50H 6:15L	12:28H 6:35L	○	1948: Author James Ellroy (L.A. Confidential) is born in Los Angeles.
64	Mon	5	6:36	6:07	11/31	1:12H 6:52L	1:06H 7:01L	○	1966: Bob Seagren vaults 17 feet, an indoor world record.
65	Tues	6	6:34	6:08	11/34	1:33H 7:28L	1:44H 7:28L	☽	1865: Explorer Alexander Hamilton Willard dies.
66	Wed	7	6:33	6:09	11/36	1:55H 8:05L	2:25H 7:55L	☽	1876 Alexander Graham Bell is granted a patent for the telephone.
67	Thurs	8	6:32	6:10	11/38	2:17H 8:46L	3:11H 8:22L	☽	1968: Student protest: the Chicano Blowout happens.
68	Fri	9	6:30	6:11	11/41	2:44H 9:32L	4:05H 8:53L	☽	1842: Gold is discovered in Placerita Canyon.
69	Sat	10	6:29	6:12	11/43	3:17H 10:26L	5:18H 9:31L	☽	1933: An earthquake in Long Beach kills 120 people.
70	Sun	11	6:27	6:13	11/46	4:59H	12:31L 7:58H 11:24L	◑	1889: The Whittier State School is established.
71	Mon	12	6:26	6:14	11/48	5:56H	1:42L 9:13H	◑	1928: Part of the St. Francis Dam collapses, killing over 450.
72	Tues	13	6:24	6:15	11/51	12:44L 7:09H	2:50L 10:28H	●	1897: San Diego State University is founded.
73	Wed	14	6:23	6:16	11/53	2:13L 8:27H	3:48L 11:07H	●	1910: The oil rig Lakeview Gusher starts blowing 100,000 barrels a day.
74	Thurs	15	6:21	6:17	11/56	3:27L 9:38H	4:36L 11:39H	●	1848: Newspapers report gold discovery; it is not believed.
75	Fri	16	6:20	6:18	11/58	4:28L 10:39H	5:19L	●	1774: Explorer Juan Bautista de Anza leads the first party through the DeAnza Pass.

The afternoon is bright,
with spring in the air,
a mild March afternoon, ...
I am alone in the quiet patio
looking for some old untried illusion—
some shadow on the whiteness of the wall
some memory asleep
on the stone rim of the fountain ...

—ANTONIO MACHADO (1875–1939),
SELECTED POEMS, # 3, TRANSLATED BY ALAN S. TRUEBLOOD

DAY / YEAR	DAY / WEEK	DAY / MONTH	SUN RISE	SUN SET	LENGTH OF DAY	TIDE AM	TIDE PM	MOON	ON THIS DAY
76	Sat	17	6:18	6:19	12/01	12:09H 5:22L 11:35H	5:59L	●	1950: Univ. California-Berkeley researchers create element 98, "Californium"
77	Sun	18	6:17	6:20	12/03	12:39H 6:12L	12:29H 6:37L	●	1848: San Francisco population is 575 males, 177 females, 60 children.
78	Mon	19	6:15	6:21	12/06	1:10H 7:01L	1:22H 7:14L	●	1851: *The Sacramento Union* is first published.
79	Tues	20	6:14	6:21	12/07	1:42H 7:50L	2:16H 7:252L	●	2005: Condoleezza Rice arrives in Beijing, China.
80	Wed	21	6:12	6:22	12/10	2:17H 8:41L	3:13H 8:31L	●	1963: Alcatraz Island is closed.
81	Thurs	22	6:11	6:23	12/12	2:54H 9:34L	4:13H 9:12L	●	1957: Daly City is epicenter of 5.3 magnitude earthquake.
82	Fri	23	6:09	6:24	12/15	3:36H 10:30L	5:22H 9:58L	◗	1868: University of California is chartered.
83	Sat	24	6:08	6:25	12/17	4:24H 11:34L	6:44H 10:55L	◖	1973: 1st ever professional track meet held in Los Angeles.
84	Sun	25	6:06	6:26	12/20	5:21H	12:43L 8:12H	◐	2006: Over 500,000 protest federal immigration legislation in L.A.
85	Mon	26	6:04	6:27	12/23	12:09L 6:34H	1:57L 9:28H	◐	1874: Poet Robert Frost born in San Francisco.
86	Tues	27	6:03	6:28	12/25	1:41L 7:57H	3:04L 10:23H	◑	1850: San Jose becomes first incorporated city in California.
87	Wed	28	6:01	6:30	12/29	3:05L 9:15H	4:00L 11:06H	◔	1776: Site for Presidio is established in San Francisco.
88	Thurs	29	6:00	6:30	12/30	4:10L 10:19H	4:46L 11:41H	◖	1971: Death penalty recommended for Charles Manson and three followers.
89	Fri	30	5:58	6:31	12/33	5:02L 11:13H	5:24L	◗	1964: TV show *Jeopardy!* makes its NBC television debut.
90	Sat	31	5:57	6:32	12/35	12:10H 5:44L	12:00H 5:57L	○	1782: San Buenaventura mission is founded.

● NEW MOON ◐ FIRST QUARTER ○ FULL MOON ◑ LAST QUARTER

DAY / YEAR	DAY / WEEK	DAY / MONTH	SUN RISE	SUN SET	LENGTH OF DAY	TIDE AM	TIDE PM	MOON	ON THIS DAY
91	Sun	1	5:55	6:33	12/38	12:35H 6:21L	12:42H 6:27L	○	1847: There are 79 buildings counted in Yerba Buena.
92	Mon	2	5:54	6:33	12/39	12:58H 6:56L	1:22H 6:55L	○	1902: First full-time electric movie theater opens in Los Angeles.
93	Tues	3	5:52	6:34	12/42	1:19H 7:30L	2:01H 7:22L	○	1848: First American public school opens in San Francisco.
94	Wed	4	5:51	6:35	12/44	1:39H 8:04L	2:41H 7:50L	○	1860: El Dorado becomes a Central Overland Pony Express station.
95	Thurs	5	5:49	6:36	12/47	2:01H 8:39L	3:22H 8:18L	○	1969: Huge antiwar demonstration held in San Francisco.
96	Fri	6	5:48	6:37	12/49	2:26H 9:18L	4:08H 8:49L	☽	1862: The Battle of Bishop Creek is fought.
97	Sat	7	5:46	6:38	12/52	2:55H 10:02L	5:02H 9:23L	☽	2003: Police fire rubber bullets at antiwar protestors at Oakland Port.
98	Sun	8	5:45	6:39	12/54	3:31H 10:53L	6:11H 10:07L	☽	1916: 3 die in Corona's Boulevard Race, its last.
99	Mon	9	5:44	6:40	12/56	4:17H 11:53L	7:32H 11:11L	☽	1967: The first Boeing 737 takes its maiden flight.
100	Tues	10	5:42	6:41	12/59	5:17H	12:58L 8:42H	◑	1970: The Beatles break up.
101	Wed	11	5:41	6:42	13/01	12:37L 6:35H	2:02L 9:32H	●	2004: Phil Mickelson wins the 68th Masters Tournament.
102	Thurs	12	5:39	6:43	13/04	2:04L 8:00H	2:59L 10:10H	●	1859: The Dogtown gold nugget is discovered at the Willard Claim.
103	Fri	13	5:38	6:43	13/05	3:16L 9:18H	3:50L 10:44H	●	1860: The first Pony Express mail arrives in San Francisco.
104	Sat	14	5:36	6:44	13/08	4:16L 10:27H	4:35L 11:17H	●	1846: The Donner Party departs Illinois for California.
105	Sun	15	5:35	6:45	13/10	5:09L 11:29H	5:18L 11:49H	●	1927: First celebrities leave footprints at Grauman's Chinese Theater.
106	Mon	16	5:34	6:46	13/12	5:59L	12:28L 5:59H	●	1977: The Apple II is introduced.

I DIDN'T KNOW THAT ALMANAC CALIFORNIA EDITION 2007

Everything is blooming most recklessly; if it were voices instead of colors, there would be an unbelievable shrieking into the heart of the night.

—RAINER MARIA RILKE (1875–1926),
SELECTED LETTERS OF RAINER MARIA RILKE

DAY / YEAR	DAY / WEEK	DAY / MONTH	SUN RISE	SUN SET	LENGTH OF DAY	TIDE AM	TIDE PM	MOON	ON THIS DAY
107	Tues	17	5:32	6:47	13/15	12:24H 6:48L	1:24H 6:40L	●	1937: Daffy Duck makes his debut in *Porky's Duck Hunt.*
108	Wed	18	5:31	6:48	13/17	1:00H 7:36L	2:20H 7:21L	●	1906: The Great San Francisco Earthquake occurs at 5:12 AM.
109	Thurs	19	5:29	6:49	13/20	1:38H 8:26L	3:18H 8:04L	●	1934: Shirley Temple makes her debut in *Stand Up and Cheer.*
110	Fri	20	5:28	6:50	13/22	2:20H 9:17L	4:18H 8:51L	●	1972: Apollo 16 lands on the moon.
111	Sat	21	5:27	6:51	13/24	3:05H 10:12L	5:24H 9:44L	●	2006: Court of appeals hears arguments in Apple Computer vs. Apple bloggers.
112	Sun	22	5:25	6:52	13/27	3:56H 11:10L	6:34H 10:49L	●	1972: Vietnam antiwar protestors demonstrate in Los Angeles.
113	Mon	23	5:24	6:53	13/29	4:47H	12:13L 7:45H	◗	1928: Shirley Temple is born in Santa Monica.
114	Tues	24	5:23	6:54	13/31	12:10L 6:10H	1:17L 8:46H	◑	1961: Bob Dylan makes his recording debut.
115	Wed	25	5:22	6:55	13/33	1:38L 7:34H	2:17L 9:35H	◑	1863: Central Pacific track reaches Junction, now called Roseville.
116	Thurs	26	5:20	6:55	13/35	2:55L 8:53H	3:10L 10:14H	◖	2006: UCSD researcher Tim Gentner discovers songbirds are capable of learning simple grammar.
117	Fri	27	5:19	6:56	13/37	3:55L 10:00H	3:55L 10:47H	◖	1859: Pioneer Peter Lassen killed by Indians.
118	Sat	28	5:18	6:57	13/39	4:43L 10:58H	4:34L 11:16H	◖	2003: Apple's iTunes Music Stores launches.
119	Sun	29	5:17	6:58	13/41	5:24L 11:49H	5:10L 11:41H	◖	1863: William Randolph Hearst is born in San Francisco.
120	Mon	30	5:15	6:59	13/44	6:00L	12:36H 5:42L	◗	1938: Bugs Bunny introduced in cartoon short *Porky's Hare Hunt.*

● NEW MOON　◖ FIRST QUARTER　○ FULL MOON　◑ LAST QUARTER

DAY / YEAR	DAY / WEEK	DAY / MONTH	SUN RISE	SUN SET	LENGTH OF DAY	TIDE AM	TIDE PM	MOON	ON THIS DAY
121	Tues	1	5:14	7:00	13/46	12:05H 6:35L	1:19H 6:14L	○	2005: Pres. G.W. Bush lands on an aircraft carrier outside San Diego.
122	Wed	2	5:13	7:01	13/48	12:28H 7:08L	2:01H 6:45L	○	1925: San Francisco's Kezar Stadium opens.
123	Thurs	3	5:12	7:02	13/50	12:52H 7:43L	2:42H 7:16L	○	1923: McCready and Oakley end 1st transcontinental flight in San Diego.
124	Fri	4	5:11	7:03	13/52	1:19H 8:19L	3:24H 7:49L	○	1861: Civil War recruiters organize in the mining town Murphys.
125	Sat	5	5:10	7:04	13/54	1:48H 8:58L	4:10H 8:25L	○	1893: NYSE crash begins the Great Depression.
126	Sun	6	5:09	7:05	13/56	2:23H 9:41L	5:02H 9:07L	☽	1882: Chinese immigrant laborers are excluded from the U.S. for 10 years.
127	Mon	7	5:08	7:05	13/57	3:03H 10:30L	5:59H 10:01L	☽	1776: Friar Francisco Garcés first explores area of Bakersfield.
128	Tues	8	5:07	7:06	13/59	3:53H 11:22L	6:57H 11:12L	☽	1984: The USSR announces boycott of L.A. Summer Olympics.
129	Wed	9	5:06	7:07	14/01	4:55H	12:18L 7:49H	☽	1974: Impeachment hearings begin against Richard Nixon.
130	Thurs	10	5:05	7:08	14/03	12:34L 6:12H	1:13L 8:33H	◑	1910: Pilot Glenn Martin makes longest and fastest overwater flight.
131	Fri	11	5:04	7:09	14/05	1:53L 7:39H	2:08L 9:12H	●	1889: The Mussel Slough Tragedy ends with 7 dead.
132	Sat	12	5:03	7:10	14/07	3:02L 9:04H	2:59L 9:49H	●	1848: Sam Brannan sets off gold fever in San Francisco.
133	Sun	13	5:02	7:11	14/09	4:02L 10:20H	3:48L 10:27H	●	1865: Central Pacific tracks reach Auburn; Chinese laborers arrive.
134	Mon	14	5:01	7:12	14/11	4:56L 11:28H	4:35L 11:05H	●	1944: Filmmaker George Lucas is born in Modesto.
135	Tues	15	5:00	7:13	14/13	5:46L	12:31H 5:22L 11:44H	●	1929: Mickey Mouse debuts as star of silent film *Plane Crazy*.
136	Wed	16	4:59	7:13	14/14	6:35L	1:29H 6:08L	●	1848: Gold is discovered near what will become Auburn.

I DIDN'T KNOW THAT ALMANAC CALIFORNIA EDITION 2007

The month of May was come, when every lusty heart beginneth to blossom, and to bring forth fruit; for like as herbs and trees bring forth fruit and flourish in May, in likewise every lusty heart ...springeth and flourisheth ...

—SIR THOMAS MALORY
(C. 1405–1471), *LE MORTE D'ARTHUR*, 1485

DAY / YEAR	DAY / WEEK	DAY / MONTH	SUN RISE	SUN SET	LENGTH OF DAY	TIDE AM	TIDE PM	MOON	ON THIS DAY
137	Thurs	17	4:59	7:14	14/15	12:26H 7:24L	2:25H 6:55L	●	1974: Police raid home of Patty Hearst kidnappers.
138	Fri.	18	4:58	7:15	14/17	1:09H 8:13L	3:20H 7:44L	●	1926: Aimee McPherson disappears while swimming at Venice Beach.
139	Sat	19	4:57	7:16	14/19	1:55H 9:02L	4:16H 8:37L	●	1880: Robert Louis Stevenson arrives in Silverado with his bride.
140	Sun	20	4:56	7:17	14/21	2:43H 9:52L	5:12H 9:35L	●	1873: Levi Strauss and Jacob Davis receive patent for blue jeans.
141	Mon	21	4:56	7:18	14/22	3:35H 10:44L	6:09H 10:42L	●	1979: The White Night riots occur in San Francisco.
142	Tues	22	4:55	7:18	14/23	4:34H 11:36L	7:03H 11:57L	●	1915: Lassen Peak erupts, spewing a huge cloud of ash into the sky.
143	Wed	23	4:54	7:19	14/25	5:41H	12:28L 7:53H	◑	1846: U.S. declares war on Mexico.
144	Thurs	24	4:54	7:20	14/26	1:16L 6:59H	1:19L 8:36H	◑	1976: California sweeps wine competition in Paris, France.
145	Fri	25	4:53	7:21	14/28	2:28L 8:20H	2:07L 9:14H	◑	1992: Jay Leno takes over as host of the *Tonight Show*.
146	Sat	26	4:52	7:22	14/30	3:27L 9:35H	2:53L 9:47H	◖	1951: Future astronaut Sally Ride is born in Encino.
147	Sun	27	4:52	7:22	14/30	4:15L 10:42H	3:36L 10:18H	◖	1937: The Golden Gate Bridge is opened to pedestrian traffic.
148	Mon	28	4:51	7:23	14/32	4:57L 11:39H	4:17L 10:47H	◖	1892: The Sierra Club is founded.
149	Tues	29	4:51	7:24	14/33	5:36L 12:30H	4:57L 11:16H	◖	1848: *The Californian* suspends publication due to gold rush.
150	Wed	30	4:50	7:24	14/34	6:13L 5:35L	1:16H 11:46H	◖	1967: Evel Knievel jumps his motorcycle over 17 cars in Gardena.
151	Thurs	31	4:50	7:25	14/35	6:49L 6:12L	1:59H	○	1921: Comedian Buster Keaton marries actress Natalie Talmadge.

● NEW MOON ◑ FIRST QUARTER ○ FULL MOON ◖ LAST QUARTER

DAY / YEAR	DAY / WEEK	DAY / MONTH	SUN RISE	SUN SET	LENGTH OF DAY	TIDE AM	TIDE PM	MOON	ON THIS DAY
152	Fri	1	4:50	7:26	14/36	12:17H 7:25L	2:40H 6:49L	◯	1899: First commercial oil well drilled in the Kern River Oilfield.
153	Sat	2	4:49	7:26	14/37	12:50H 8:03L	3:22H 7:28L	◯	1985: Serial killer Leonard Lake arrested near San Francisco.
154	Sun	3	4:49	7:27	14/38	1:26H 8:43L	4:03H 8:11L	◯	1943: The Zoot Suit Riots erupt in Los Angeles.
155	Mon	4	4:49	7:28	14/39	2:05H 9:24L	4:46H 9:00L	◗	1876: The Transcontinental Express makes its first arrival in San Francisco.
156	Tues	5	4:48	7:28	14/40	2:50H 10:07L	5:30H 9:59L	◗	1977: The Apple II goes on sale.
157	Wed	6	4:48	7:29	14/41	3:41H 10:52L	6:12H 11:09L	◗	1968: Bobby Kennedy is assasinated in Los Angeles.
158	Thurs	7	4:48	7:30	14/42	4:43H 11:38L	6:55H	◗	1966: Ronald Reagan becomes the 22nd governor of California.
159	Fri	8	4:48	7:30	14/42	12:24L 5:59H	12:27L 7:36H	◑	1906: Pres. Theodore Roosevelt signs the Antiquities Act into law.
160	Sat	9	4:48	7:31	14/43	1:38L 7:27H	1:18L 8:18H	●	1967: The Haight-Ashbury Free Medical Clinic opens.
161	Sun	10	4:48	7:31	14/43	2:46L 8:58H	2:10L 9:00H	●	1966: Big Brother and the Holding Company preform their first gig.
162	Mon	11	4:47	7:32	14/45	3:47L 10:21H	3:04L 9:45H	●	1962: Frank Morris and John and Clarence Anglin escape Alcatraz.
163	Tues	12	4:47	7:32	14/45	4:43L 11:34H	3:59L 10:30H	●	1988: Rusty Wallace wins the last NASCAR Winston Cup race at Riverside.
164	Wed	13	4:47	7:32	14/45	5:35L	12:37H 4:53L 11:17H	●	1798: Mission San Luis Rey de Francia is founded.
165	Thurs	14	4:47	7:33	14/46	6:25L	1:33H 5:46L	●	1846: The California Republic is established.
166	Fri	15	4:47	7:33	14/46	12:04H 7:13L	2:24H 6:39L	●	1846: The Oregon boundary is set at the 49th parallel.
167	Sat	16	4:47	7:34	14/47	12:52H 8:00L	3:12H 7:32L	●	1970: Golfer Phil Mickelson is born in San Diego.

*There are moments, above all on June evenings, when the
lakes that hold our moons are sucked into the earth, and
nothing is left but wine and the touch of a hand.*

—CHARLES MORGAN (1894–1958)

DAY / YEAR	DAY / WEEK	DAY / MONTH	SUN RISE	SUN SET	LENGTH OF DAY	TIDE AM	TIDE PM	MOON	ON THIS DAY
168	Sun	17	4:48	7:34	14/46	1:40H 8:45L	3:59H 8:26L	●	1980: Tennis champion Venus Williams is born in Lynwood.
169	Mon	18	4:48	7:34	14/46	2:28H 9:29L	4:44H 9:23L	●	1967: Jimi Hendrix burns his guitar onstage at Monterey Pop Festival.
170	Tues	19	4:48	7:35	14/47	3:17H 10:12L	5:28H 10:24L	●	1919: Future film critic Pauline Kael is born.
171	Wed	20	4:48	7:35	14/47	4:09H 10:53L	6:11H 11:29L	●	1963: Final original *Leave It to Beaver* is aired.
172	Thurs	21	4:48	7:35	14/47	5:08H 11:35L	6:51H	◐	1805: Lieutenant Gabriel Moraga traversed and recorded the Pacheco Pass.
173	Fri	22	4:48	7:35	14/47	12:38L 6:18H	12:16L 7:29H	◑	1898: U.S. Marines land in Cuba during the Spanish-American War.
174	Sat	23	4:49	7:35	14/46	1:45L 7:40H	1:00L 8:07H	◑	1972: Watergate tapes are recorded.
175	Sun	24	4:49	7:35	14/46	2:46L 9:07H	1:47L 8:44H	◖	1865: Fort Téjon is established by the U.S. Army in the San Joaquin Valley.
176	Mon	25	4:49	7:36	14/47	3:39L 10:25H	2:36L 9:21H	◖	1921: A new oil field is discovered under Signal Hill, causing massive property price inflation.
177	Tues	26	4:50	7:36	14/46	4:27L 11:30H	3:27L 9:59H	◖	1945: The United Nations Charter is signed in San Francisco.
178	Wed	27	4:50	7:36	14/46	5:10L	12:23H 4:16L 10:38H	◖	1858: The Church of St. James the Apostle is founded in Oakland.
179	Thurs	28	4:50	7:36	14/46	5:51L	1:08H 5:03L 11:16H	◖	1978: The U.S. Supreme Court bars quota systems in college admissions.
180	Fri	29	4:51	7:36	14/45	6:30L	1:48H 5:47L 11:55H	○	1776: The first mass is celebrated at La Misión de San Francisco de Asis.
181	Sat	30	4:51	7:36	14/45	7:08L	2:25H 6:30L	○	1864: The Yosemite Grant is signed by Pres. Lincoln.

● NEW MOON   ◑ FIRST QUARTER   ○ FULL MOON   ◐ LAST QUARTER

DAY / YEAR	DAY / WEEK	DAY / MONTH	SUN RISE	SUN SET	LENGTH OF DAY	TIDE AM	TIDE PM	MOON	ON THIS DAY
182	Sun	1	4:52	7:36	14/44	12:34H 7:46L	3:01H 7:15L	○	1993: John Luigi Ferri kills eight and wounds six before committing suicide in San Francisco.
183	Mon	2	4:52	7:35	14/43	1:15H 8:24L	3:36H 8:02L	○	1857: The first school is built in Plumas County for 19 children.
184	Tues	3	4:52	7:35	14/43	1:58H 9:01L	4:10H 8:54L	○	1852: The 2nd U.S. Mint is established in San Francisco.
185	Wed	4	4:53	7:35	14/42	2:45H 9:39L	4:45H 9:53L	☽	1823: La Misión de San Francisco Solano de Sonoma is founded.
186	Thurs	5	4:54	7:35	14/41	3:38H 10:19L	5:22H 10:57L	☽	1934: Bloody Thursday riots erupt during San Francisco maritime strike.
187	Fri	6	4:54	7:35	14/41	4:40H 11:00L	6:01H	◑	1946: The bikini bathing suit is created.
188	Sat	7	4:55	7:34	14/39	12:06L 5:55H 11:44L	6:44H	◑	1846: The American flag is raised at Monterey by Commodore John Sloat.
189	Sun	8	4:55	7:34	14/39	1:18L 7:25H	12:34L 7:30H	●	1932: The Dow Jones Industrial Average reaches its lowest level.
190	Mon	9	4:56	7:34	14/38	2:28L 9:02H	1:29L 8:21H	●	1995: The Grateful Dead perform their last concert ever.
191	Tues	10	4:56	7:34	14/38	3:32L 10:30H	2:32L 9:15H	●	1852: A Visalia election occurs at Charter Oak.
192	Wed	11	4:57	7:33	14/36	4:32L 11:41H	3:36L 10:09H	●	1967: Rudolph Nureyev is arrested in Haight-Ashbury for possession of marijuana.
193	Thurs	12	4:58	7:33	14/35	5:25L	12:38H 4:39L 11:03H	●	Kristi Yamaguchi is born in Hayward.
194	Fri	13	4:58	7:32	14/34	6:15L	1:26H 5:38L 11:55H	●	1895: The Sacramento Electric Power and Light Company opens for business.
195	Sat	14	4:59	7:32	14/33	7:01L	2:09H 6:32L	●	1769: Spanish explorer Gaspar de Portola discovers Monterey Bay.
196	Sun	15	5:00	7:31	14/31	12:44H 7:43L	2:49H 7:23L	●	2005: Disneyland "relaunches" Space Mountain.
197	Mon	16	5:01	7:31	14/30	1:30H 8:22L	3:26H 8:14L	●	1769: Mission San Diego de Alcalá is established.

I DIDN'T KNOW THAT ALMANAC CALIFORNIA EDITION 2007

July 4. Statistics show that we lose more fools on this day
than in all the other days of the year put together.
This proves, by the number left in stock, that one Fourth of
July per year is now inadequate, the country has grown so.

*—*MARK TWAIN (1835–1910)

DAY / YEAR	DAY / WEEK	DAY / MONTH	SUN RISE	SUN SET	LENGTH OF DAY	TIDE AM	TIDE PM	MOON	ON THIS DAY
198	Tues	17	5:01	7:30	14/29	2:15H 8:59L	4:02H 9:04L	●	1955: Disneyland opens in Anaheim.
199	Wed	18	5:02	7:30	14/28	3:00H 9:34L	4:35H 9:56L	●	1984: James Huberty kills 21 at a McDonald's in San Ysidro.
200	Thurs	19	5:03	7:29	14/26	3:46H 10:07L	5:08H 10:50L	●	2005: Death Valley records a temperature of 129F.
201	Fri	20	5:03	7:28	14/25	4:03H 10:41L	5:41H 11:49L	●	1920: Boxer Jack Johnson is arrested near San Diego after 5 years on the run.
202	Sat	21	5:04	7:28	14/24	5;42H 11:17L	6:15H	◗	1969: Neil Armstrong and Buzz Aldrin walk on the moon.
203	Sun	22	5:05	7:27	14/22	12:51L 7:02H 11:57L	6:54H	◑	1916: A bomb explodes near the Ferry Building in San Francisco, killing 10.
204	Mon	23	5:06	7:26	14/20	1:55L 8:38H	12:44L 7:38H	◖	1936: Supreme Court Justice Anthony Kennedy is born in Sacramento.
205	Tues	24	5:07	7:26	14/19	2:57L 10:07H	1:42L 8:27H	◖	1956: Dean Martin and Jerry Lewis perform their last comedy show together.
206	Wed	25	5:07	7:25	14/18	3:52L 11:16H	2:46L 9:19H	◖	1853: Bandit Joaquin Murieta is killed by a posse of state rangers.
207	Thurs	26	5:08	7:24	14/16	4:42L	12:05H 3:47L 10:09H	◖	1878: Black Bart makes his last clean getaway from a Wells Fargo stagecoach.
208	Fri	27	5:09	7:23	14/14	5:26L	12:45H 4:41L 10:56H	◗	1964: U.S. forces in Vietnam reach 21,000.
209	Sat	28	5:10	7:22	14/12	6:07L	1:20H 5:30L 11:40H	◗	1865: The Pacific Mail steamer *Brother Jonathan* is wrecked in a storm at St. George's Reef near Crescent City.
210	Sun	29	5:11	7:21	14/10	6:45L	1:51H 6:17L	○	1849: Mass meeting held on Yuba River to ban slaves from mines.
211	Mon	30	5:11	7:20	14/09	12:24H 7:21L	2:22H 7:04L	○	1932: Opening ceremonies of Summer Olympics in Los Angeles.
212	Tues	31	5:12	7:19	14/07	1:08H 7:57L	2:52H 7:52L	○	1976: NASA releases the famous Face on Mars photo taken by Viking 1.

● NEW MOON ◑ FIRST QUARTER ○ FULL MOON ◐ LAST QUARTER

DAY / YEAR	DAY / WEEK	DAY / MONTH	SUN RISE	SUN SET	LENGTH OF DAY	TIDE AM	TIDE PM	MOON	ON THIS DAY
213	Wed	1	5:13	7:18	14/05	1:54H 8:32L	3:22H 8:44L	○	2003: The Martin Luther King Jr. Library opens at San Jose State.
214	Thurs	2	5:14	7:18	14/04	2:43H 9:08L	3:55H 9:39L	☽	2003: A condo under construction in San Diego is suspiciously destroyed.
215	Fri	3	5:15	7:16	14/01	3:38H 9:45L	4:31H 10:39L	☽	1977: Al Arnold begins 192 mile walk from Death Valley to Mt. Whitney.
216	Sat	4	5:16	7:15	13/59	4:42H 10:24L	5:11H 11:45L	☽	1985: Angels' Rod Carew hits 3000th career hit.
217	Sun	5	5:17	7:14	13/57	5:59H 11:08L	5:57H	◑	1962: Marilyn Monroes dies of probable drug overdose in Los Angeles.
218	Mon	6	5:17	7:13	13/56	12:56L 7:33H	12:00L 6:51H	◑	1997: Microsoft buys $150 million of ailing Apple Computer stock.
219	Tues	7	5:18	7:12	13/54	2:09L 9:13H	1:04L 7:53H	●	1967: Beatle George Harrison visits Haight-Ashbury in San Francisco.
220	Wed	8	5:19	7:11	13/52	3:18L 10:36H	2:20L 8:59H	●	1937: Dustin Hoffman is born in Los Angeles.
221	Thurs	9	5:20	7:10	13/50	4:20L 11:37H	3:35L 10:03H	●	1995: Grateful Dead's Jerry Garcia dies in Forest Knolls.
222	Fri	10	5:21	7:09	13/48	5:14L	12:24H 4:41L 11:01H	●	1870: California's first Grange Hall is organized near Pilot Hill.
223	Sat	11	5:22	7:08	13.46	6:00L	1:04H 5:38L 11:52H	●	1965: The Watts Riots begin and last for five days, causing $35 million of property damage.
224	Sun	12	5:23	7:06	13/43	6:42L	1:40H 6:27L	●	2004: California Supreme Court annuls same-sex marriages in San Francisco.
225	Mon	13	5:23	7:05	13/42	12:39H 7:18L	2:12H 7:13L	●	1812: Fort Ross is dedicated.
226	Tues	14	5:24	7:04	13/40	1:22H 7:51L	2:41H 7:57L	●	1925: Hetch Hetchy Moccasin Powerhouse is completed and goes on line.
227	Wed	15	5:25	7:03	13/38	2:04H 8:22L	3:08H 8:39L	●	1846: California's first American newspaper is established in Monterey.
228	Thurs	16	5:26	7:01	13/35	2:45H 8:52L	3:34H 9:22L	●	1942: The crew of the U.S. naval blimp L-8 disappear while in flight.

In the parching August wind,
Cornfields bow the head,
Sheltered in round valley depths,
On low hills outspread.

— Christina Georgina Rossetti (1830–1894),
A Year's Windfalls

DAY / YEAR	DAY / WEEK	DAY / MONTH	SUN RISE	SUN SET	LENGTH OF DAY	TIDE AM	TIDE PM	MOON	ON THIS DAY
229	Fri	17	5:27	7:00	13/33	3:29H 9:21L	4:00H 10:08L	●	1953: First meeting of Narcotics Anonymous is held in California.
230	Sat	18	5:28	6:59	13/31	4:17H 9:52L	4:29H 10:59L	●	1936: Robert Redford is born in Santa Monica.
231	Sun	19	5:29	6:58	13/29	5:15H 10:24L	5:01H 11:56L	◐	1848: *New York Herald* reports discovery of gold in California.
232	Mon	20	5:29	6:56	13/27	6:32H 11:02L	5:41H	◑	1989: Lyle and Erik Menendez shoot and kill their parents.
233	Tues	21	5:30	6:55	13/25	1:01L 8:12H 11:52L	6:34H	◑	1971: Black Panther George Jackson shot and killed in prison yard.
234	Wed	22	5:31	6:54	13/23	2:10L 9:47H	1:01L 7:38H	◑	1861: Samuel Bishop establishes St. Francis Ranch in Owens Valley.
235	Thurs	23	5:32	6:52	13/20	3:14L 10:50H	2:19L 8:44H	◑	1977: Visalian Allen wins 1st Kremer prize in Kern County.
236	Fri	24	5:33	6:51	13/18	4:08L 11:33H	3:28L 9:45H	◖	1932: Amerlia Earhart flies nonstop from Los Angeles to Newark, N.J.
237	Sat	25	5:34	6:49	13/15	4:55L	12:06H 4:26L 10:38H	◖	1991: Linus Torvalds announces he is working on a new, free computer operating system.
238	Sun	26	5:35	6:48	13/13	5:35L	12:36H 5:16L 11:27H	◖	1920: The 19th Amendment gives women the right to vote.
239	Mon	27	5:35	6:47	13/12	6:13L	1:04H 6:04L	○	1883: Krakatoa eruption in Indonesia is felt worldwide..
240	Tues	28	5:36	6:45	13/09	12:15H 6:48L	1:32H 6:51L	○	1784: Fr. Junipero Serra dies at Mission Carmel and is buried there.
241	Wed	29	5:37	6:44	13/07	1:02H 7:23L	2:01H 7:39L	○	1966: The Beatles give their last public performance at Candlestick Park.
242	Thurs	30	5:38	6:42	13/04	1:52H 7:58L	2:32H 8:29L	○	1952: Baseball great Ted Williams is born in San Diego.
243	Fri	31	5:39	6:41	13/02	2:44H 8:34L	3:06H 9:22L	◗	1908: Author William Sayoran is born in San Franciso.

● NEW MOON　◐ FIRST QUARTER　○ FULL MOON　◑ LAST QUARTER

DAY / YEAR	DAY / WEEK	DAY / MONTH	SUN RISE	SUN SET	LENGTH OF DAY	TIDE AM	TIDE PM	MOON	ON THIS DAY
244	Sat	1	5:40	6:39	12/59	3:42H 9:12L	3:43H 10:19L	☽	1772: Mission San Luis Obispo is established.
245	Sun	2	5:41	6:38	12/57	4:48H 9:53L	4:26H 11:23L	☽	2003: An accident at Disneyland Park claims the life of one man.
246	Mon	3	5:41	6:36	12/55	6:08H 10:41L	5:18H	☽	1852: The first synagogue on the Pacific Coast is dedicated in Sacramento.
247	Tues	4	5:42	6:35	12/53	12:33H 7:42H 11:42L	6:21H	◑	1781: Los Angeles is founded by a group of 44 Spanish settlers.
248	Wed	5	5:43	6:33	12/50	1:48L 9:14H	1:02L 7:36H	●	1922: Sarah Winchester dies and construction on her mansion ceases.
249	Thurs	6	5:44	6:32	12/48	3:00L 10:23H	2:29L 8:53H	●	1869: The first westbound train arrives in San Francisco.
250	Fri	7	5:45	6:30	12/45	4:01L 11:13H	3:45L 10:01H	●	2005: Governor Schwarzenegger vetoes same-sex marriage bill.
251	Sat	8	5:46	6:29	12/43	4:53L 11:54H	4:45L 10:59L	●	1965: The Delano Grape Strike begins and lasts for five years.
252	Sun	9	5:46	6:27	12/41	5:35L	12:28H 5:35L 11:49H	●	1850: California is admitted to the Union as the thirty-first state.
253	Mon	10	5:47	6:26	12/39	6:12L	12:58H 6:19L	●	1870: Newport Bay opens for commerce.
254	Tues	11	5:48	6:24	12/36	12:33H 6:45L	1:25H 6:59L	●	1886: The Order of Native Daughters of the Golden West is organized.
255	Wed	12	5:49	6:23	12/34	1:15H 7:14L	1:49H 7:36L	●	1862: Camp Lincoln is established near Crsecent City.
256	Thurs	13	5:50	6:21	12/31	1:55H 7:42L	2:12H 8:13L	●	2004: Metro-Goldwyn-Mayer accepts a $3 billion take-over bid from Sony.
257	Fri	14	5:51	6:19	12/28	2:35H 8:10L	2:34H 8:51L	●	1969: Sept. 14th is the first birthdate draw of the Vietnam War draft.
258	Sat	15	5:51	6:18	12/27	3:18H 8:38L	2:57H 9:31L	●	1997: Larry Page and Sergey Brin register the domain name Google.com.
259	Sun	16	5:52	6:16	12/24	4:04H 9:08L	3:24H 10:16L	●	1901: Alturas is incorporated as the only city in Modoc County.

By all these lovely tokens
September days are here,
With summer's best of weather
And autumn's best of cheer.

—HELEN HUNT JACKSON
(1830-1885), *SEPTEMBER*

DAY / YEAR	DAY / WEEK	DAY / MONTH	SUN RISE	SUN SET	LENGTH OF DAY	TIDE AM	TIDE PM	MOON	ON THIS DAY
260	Mon	17	5:53	6:15	12/22	5:00H 9:40L	3:57H 11:09L	●	1804: Mission Santa Inés is founded in what is now Solvang.
261	Tues	18	5:54	6:13	12/19	6:13H 10:19L	4:39H	●	1882: The Pacific Stock Exchange opens in San Francisco.
262	Wed	19	5:55	6:12	12/17	12:11L 7:48H	5L36H 11:16L	◑	1952: Charlie Chaplin is barred from returning to Hollywood after a trip to England.
263	Thurs	20	5:56	6:10	12/14	1:21L 9:13H	12:38L 6:51H	◑	1818: Santa Ysabel Asistencia is consecrated by Father Fernando Martin.
264	Fri	21	5:57	5:09	12/12	2:28L 10:07H	2:04L 8:10H	◐	1970: *Monday Night Football* premieres with Howard Cosell in the booth.
265	Sat	22	5:57	6:07	12/10	3:25L 10:45H	3:14L 9:20H	◐	1975: Sara Jane Moore attempts to assassinate Pres. Gerald Ford.
266	Sun	23	5:58	6:05	12/07	4:12L 11:15H	4:12L 10:20H	◐	1849: Camp Salvation for refugees is established at Calexico.
267	Mon	24	5:59	6:04	12/05	4:54L 11:44H	5:02L 11:15H	○	1855: The preserved heads of Three-Fingered Jack and Joaquin Murieta are sold at auction for $36.
268	Tues	25	6:00	6:02	12/02	5:32L	12:12H 5:50L	○	1988: Fr. Junipero Serra is beatified by Pope John Paul II.
269	Wed	26	6:01	6:01	12/00	12:07H 6:09L	12:41H 6:37L	○	1923: The San Francisco Opera gives its first performance (*La Bohème*).
270	Thurs	27	6:02	5:59	11/57	1:00H 6:46L	1:12H 7:25L	○	1996: Riots break out in San Francisco when a white policeman kills an African-American youth.
271	Fri	28	6:03	5:58	11/55	1:53H 7:23L	1:45H 8:13L	○	1542: Juan Rodríguez Cabrillo steps onshore at San Diego harbor.
272	Sat	29	6:03	5:56	11/53	2:48H 8:02L	2:22H 9:05L	☽	2005: A wildfire in S. California burns 17,000 acres.
273	Sun	30	6:04	5:55	11/51	3:48H 8:43L	3:03H 10:00L	☽	1975: The Hughes AH-64 Apache makes its first flight.

● NEW MOON   ◐ FIRST QUARTER   ○ FULL MOON   ◑ LAST QUARTER

DAY / YEAR	DAY / WEEK	DAY / MONTH	SUN RISE	SUN SET	LENGTH OF DAY	TIDE AM	TIDE PM	MOON	ON THIS DAY
274	Mon	1	6:05	5:53	11/48	4:55H 9:29L	3:51H 11:02L	☽	1891: Stanford University opens to 599 students and 15 faculty members.
275	Tues	2	6:06	5:52	11/46	6:14H 10:26L	4:48H	☽	1962: Johnny Carson debuts at the host of the *Tonight Show*.
276	Wed	3	6:07	5:50	11/43	12:10H 7:39H 11:40L	6:00H	◐	1995: O.J. Simpson found not guilty of the murder of his wife, Nicole Brown Simpson.
277	Thurs	4	6:08	5:49	11/41	1:23L 8:55H	1:11L 7:24H	●	1850: Peter Lassen and J.G. Bruff discover Honey Lake.
278	Fri	5	6:09	5:47	11/38	2:31L 9:52H	2:39L 8:45H	●	1953: Earl Warren appointed 14th Chief Justice by Pres. Eisenhower.
279	Sat	6	6:10	5:46	11/36	3:29L 10:36H	3:47L 9:55H	●	1880: The 1st building on the Univ. of Southern California opens its doors.
280	Sun	7	6:11	5:44	11/33	4:18L 11:13H	4:41L 10:53H	●	2003: Arnold Schwarzenegger is elected governor in a special recall election.
281	Mon	8	6:11	5:43	11/32	4:58L 11:44H	5:26L 11:43H	●	1846: The Battle of Dominguez Ranch.
282	Tues	9	6:12	5:41	11/29	5:33L	12:11H 6:05L	●	1791: Mission Nuestra Señora de la Soledad is founded.
283	Wed	10	6:13	5:40	11/27	12:28H 6:05L	12:32H 6:41L	●	1911: California senate passes women's suffrage 9 years before the nation.
284	Thurs	11	6:14	5:38	11/24	1:10H 6:34L	12:57H 7:15L	●	1906: Japanese students are ordered to be taught in racially segregated schools.
285	Fri	12	6:15	5:37	11/22	1:51H 7:03L	1:19H 7:49L	●	1933: Alcatraz Island becomes a federal prison.
286	Sat	13	6:16	5:35	11/19	2:32H 7:32L	1:41H 8:24L	●	1849: The state motto "Eureka" is adopted.
287	Sun	14	6:17	5:34	11/17	3:13H 8:01L	2:06H 9:02L	●	1967: Joan Baez is arrested in Oakland for blocking a draft induction center.
288	Mon	15	6:18	5:33	11/15	4:00H 8:32L	2:35H 9:45L	●	2005: USC defeats Notre Dame 34-31 using the "Bush Push."
289	Tues	16	6:19	5:31	11/12	4:54H 9:08L	3:130H 10:34L	●	1923: The Walt Disney Company is founded.

There is no season when such pleasant and sunny

spots may be lighted on, and produce so pleasant an

effect on the feelings, as now in October ...

—NATHANIEL HAWTHORNE (1804–1864)

DAY / YEAR	DAY / WEEK	DAY / MONTH	SUN RISE	SUN SET	LENGTH OF DAY	TIDE AM	TIDE PM	MOON	ON THIS DAY
290	Wed	17	6:20	7:30	11/10	6:01H 9:53L	3:54H 11:32L	●	1904: The Bank of Italy opens in a San Francisco saloon.
291	Thurs	18	6:21	5:28	11/07	7:18H 10:58L	4:52H	●	1969: Jefferson Airplane member Paul Kantner is charged with possession of marijuana.
292	Fri	19	6:22	5:27	11/05	12:34L 8:24H	12:24L 6:09H	◐	1935: The League of Nations enacts economic sanctions on fascist Italy.
293	Sat	20	6:23	5:26	11/03	1:35L 9:11H	1:49L 7:35H	◐	1991: The Oakland Hills firestorm kills 25 and destroys 3,469 homes.
294	Sun	21	6:24	5:25	11/01	2:32L 9:47H	2:59L 8:55H	◗	1985: San Francisco Councilman Dan White commits suicide after his release from prison.
295	Mon	22	6:25	5:23	10/58	3:22L 10:18H	3:57L 10:04H	◗	1986: Pres. Ronald Reagan signs the Tax Reform Act into law.
296	Tues	23	6:26	5:22	10/56	4:06L 10:49H	4:48L 11:06H	◗	1929: The New York Stock Exchange begins to show signs of panic.
297	Wed	24	6:27	5:21	10/54	4:48L 11:21H	5:36L	◖	1947: Walt Disney testifies before the House Unamerican Activities Committee.
298	Thurs	25	6:28	5:19	10/51	12:04H	6:23L 5:29L 11:54H	○	1923: The U.S. Senate begins investigating the Teapot Dome scandal.
299	Fri	26	6:29	5:18	11/49	1:00H 6:10L	12:30H 7:11L	○	1861: The Central Overland Pony Express discontinues service.
300	Sat	27	6:30	5:17	11/47	1:56H 6:51L	1:08H 7:59L	○	2002: The Anaheim Angels win baseball's World Series.
301	Sun	28	6:31	5:16	11/45	2:53H 7:35L	1:50H 8:50L	○	1868: Thomas Edison applies for his first patent, the electric vote recorder.
302	Mon	29	6:32	5:15	11/43	3:52H 8:22L	2:35H 9:44L	◑	1969: ARPANET, the world's first electronic computer network, is established.
303	Tues	30	6:33	5:14	11/41	4:56H 9:15L	3:27H 10:42L	◑	1966: The Zodiac Killer claims his first victim, 18-year-old Cheri Jo Bates.
304	Wed	31	6:34	7:12	11/38	6:05H 10:20L	4:26H 11:43L	◑	1941: Ansel Adams photographs the moonrise over Hernandez, NM.

● NEW MOON   ◐ FIRST QUARTER   ○ FULL MOON   ◑ LAST QUARTER

DAY / YEAR	DAY / WEEK	DAY / MONTH	SUN RISE	SUN SET	LENGTH OF DAY	TIDE AM	TIDE PM	MOON	ON THIS DAY
305	Thurs	1	6:35	7:11	11/36	7:15H 11:41L	5:39H	◑	1769: The entrance to San Francisco Bay is discovered by Sergeant Jose Ortega.
306	Fri	2	6:36	5:10	11/34	12:47L 8:16H	1:11L 7:03H	●	Donner Party crossing the Sierras is trapped by a snowstorm.
307	Sat	3	6:37	5:09	11/32	1:47L 9:07H	2:32L 8:27H	●	1969: Pres. Richard M. Nixon asks the "silent majority" to join him in solidarity.
308	Sun	4	6:38	5:08	11/30	1:42L 8:48H	2:36L 8:40H	●	1920: Brand Park is given to the city of Los Angeles for a park.
309	Mon	5	6:39	5:07	11/28	2:29L 9:23H	3:27L 9:42H	●	1913: The great Los Angeles-Owens River Aqueduct is completed.
310	Tues	6	6:40	5:06	11/26	3:11L 9:54H	4:09L 10:36H	●	1939: *The Hedda Hopper Show* debuts with Hollywood gossip Hopper as host.
311	Wed	7	6:41	5:05	11/24	3:48L 10:21H	4:47L 11:24H	●	1962: Richard M. Nixon loses the gubernatorial election in California.
312	Thurs	8	6:42	5:04	11/22	4:23L 10:46H	5:21L	●	1787: Father Fermín Francisco de Lasuén founds La Purísima Concepción.
313	Fri	9	6:43	5:03	11/20	12:09H 4:56L 11:11H	5:55L	●	1969: "Indians of All Tribes" under the leadership of Richard Oakes occupy Alcatraz to claim the island.
314	Sat	10	6:44	5:03	11/19	12:51H 5:28L 11:36H	6:29L	●	1992: Diane Feinstein elected to fill the Senate seat vacated by Pete Wilson's election to governor.
315	Sun	11	6:46	5:02	11/16	1:32H 6:00L	12:02H 7:04L	●	1885: George S. Patton Jr. is born in San Gabriel.
316	Mon	12	6:47	5:01	11/14	2:14H 6:33L	12:31H 7:42L	●	1936: The San Francisco-Oakland Bay Bridge opens for traffic.
317	Tues	13	6:48	5:00	11/12	2:58H 7:08L	1:04H 8:23L	●	1849: Peter H. Burnett is elected governor.
318	Wed	14	6:49	4:59	11/10	3:47H 7:49L	1:43H 9:09L	●	1971: Mariner 9 reaches Mars, becoming the first spacecraft to orbit another planet.
319	Thurs	15	6:50	4:59	11/09	4:40H 8:41L	2:28H 9:57L	●	1870: E. H. Dyer begins to process beets at his factory in Union City.
320	Fri	16	6:51	4:58	11/07	5:35H 9:49L	3:25H 10:49L	●	1846: American forces clashed with the Spanish in the Battle of Natividad.

I DIDN'T KNOW THAT ALMANAC CALIFORNIA EDITION 2007

The wild gander leads his flock through the cool night,
Ya-honk! he says, and sounds it down to me like an invitation:
The pert may suppose it meaningless, but I listen closer,
I find its purpose and place up there toward the November sky.

—WALT WHITMAN (1819–1892),
I CELEBRATE MYSELF

DAY / YEAR	DAY / WEEK	DAY / MONTH	SUN RISE	SUN SET	LENGTH OF DAY	TIDE AM	TIDE PM	MOON	ON THIS DAY
321	Sat	17	6:52	4:57	11/05	6:24H 11:10L	4:38H 11:43L	◑	1944: Major league baseball pitcher Tom Seaver born in Fresno.
322	Sun	18	6:53	4:57	11/04	7:07H	12:30L 6:05H	◖	1849: First tuition-free public school in San Francisco opens.
323	Mon	19	6:54	4:56	11/02	12:36L 7:45H	1:39L 7:34H	◖	1924: Famous silent film director Thomas Ince dies of a heart attack.
324	Tues	20	6:55	4:55	11/00	1:27L 8:21H	2:38L 8:53H	◖	1982: Cal scores the winning touchdown in the final seconds of a Stanford game.
325	Wed	21	6:56	4:55	10/59	2:16L 8:58H	3:31L 10:03H	◖	1855: The first statewide convention of the California Colored Citizens is held.
326	Thurs	22	6:56	4:54	10/58	3:05L 9:36H	4:22L 11:07H	◖	1935: Pan American World Airways' China Clipper begins ocean airmail service.
327	Fri	23	6:58	4:54	10/56	3:52L 10:16H	5:10L	◖	1936: The first edition of *Life* magazine is published.
328	Sat	24	6:59	4:53	10/54	12:05H 4:39L 10:58H	5:59L	○	1793: English explorer George Vancouver discovers and names Point Dume.
329	Sun	25	7:00	4:53	10/53	1:00H	6:48L 5:27L 11:43H	○	1963: President John F. Kennedy is buried at Arlington National Cemetery.
330	Mon	26	7:01	4:53	10/52	1:54H 6:17L	12:29L 7:37H	○	1985: Pres. Ronald Reagan accepts a record $3 million from Random House to write his autobiography.
331	Tues	27	7:02	4:52	10/50	2:48H 7:09L	1:18H 8:27L	◗	1978: Harvey Milk and George Moscone are assassinated by Dan White.
332	Wed	28	7:03	4:52	10/49	3:43H 8:07L	2:10H 9:18L	◗	1848: *USS Lexington* departs San Francisco with $500,000 in gold.
333	Thurs	29	7:04	4:52	10/48	4:39H 9:13L	3:08H 10:09L	◗	1777: El Pueblo de San José de Guadalupe is founded by José Moraga.
334	Fri	30	7:05	4:51	10/46	5:33H 10:29L	4:14H 11:01L	◗	2004: Longtime *Jeopardy!* champion Ken Jennings finally loses, leaving him with winnings of $2,520,700, the largest ever.

● NEW MOON   ◐ FIRST QUARTER   ○ FULL MOON   ◑ LAST QUARTER

DAY / YEAR	DAY / WEEK	DAY / MONTH	SUN RISE	SUN SET	LENGTH OF DAY	TIDE AM	TIDE PM	MOON	ON THIS DAY
335	Sat	1	7:06	4:51	10/45	6:24H 11:49L	5:31H 11:51L		1981: AIDS is first identified.
336	Sun	2	7:07	4:51	10/44	7:10H	10:06L 6:56H		1845: President James K. Polk propounds Manifest Destiny.
337	Mon	3	7:08	4:51	10/43	12:41L 7:51H	2:10L 8:18H		1964: Police arrest over 800 students at the University of California–Berkeley.
338	Tues	4	7:09	4:51	10/42	1:29L 8:28H	3:02L 9:29H		1786: Mission Santa Barbara is founded by Father Fermín Francisco de Lasuén.
339	Wed	5	7:10	4:51	10/41	2:16L 9:01H	3:46L 10:30H		1941: John Steinbeck's book *Sea of Cortez* is published.
340	Thurs	6	7:11	4:51	10/40	3:00L 9:33H	4:25L 11:22H		1969: Meredith Hunter killed by Hell's Angels during Stones' concert at Altamont.
341	Fri	7	7:12	4:51	10/39	3:42L 10:04H	5:02L		1941: At Pearl Harbor, San Jose State football team helps the Honolulu Police.
342	Sat	8	7:12	4:51	10/39	12:08H 4:22L 10:35H	5:38L		1822: La Iglesia de Nuestra Señora la Reina de Los Angeles is dedicated.
343	Sun	9	7:13	4:51	10/38	12:49H 5:00L 11:06H	6:14L		1985: Steve Jobs purchases George Lucas's computer development unit and renames it Pixar Studios.
344	Mon	10	7:14	4:51	10/37	1:29H 5:37L 11:39H	6:50L		1965: The Grateful Dead play their first concert, at the Fillmore in San Francisco.
345	Tues	11	7:15	4:51	10/36	2:07H 6:15L	12:13H 7:27L		1941: The FBI detains 1,370 Japanese-Americans.
346	Wed	12	7:16	4:51	10/35	2:46H 6:55L	12:50H 8:05L		1903: The city of Fairfield is incorporated.
347	Thurs	13	7:16	4:51	10/35	3:24H 7:41L	1:#0H 8:44L		2003: California approves Gov. Arnold Schwarzenegger's $15 billion bond issue.
348	Fri	14	7:17	4:52	10/35	4:03H 8:35L	2:16H 9:24L		1817: Mission San Rafael Arcángel is founded by Father Vicente de Sarría.
349	Sat	15	7:18	4:52	10/34	4:43H 9:39L	3:11H 10:07L		1966: Walt Disney dies of lung cancer after a lifelong smoking habit.
350	Sun	16	7:18	4:52	10/34	5:22H 10:51L	4:20H 10:52L		1931: The Art Deco style Paramount Theatre opens on Broadway in Oakland.

I DIDN'T KNOW THAT ALMANAC CALIFORNIA EDITION 2007

"We are nearer to Spring
Than we were in September."
I heard a bird sing
In the dark of December.

—OLIVER HERFORD (1863–1935),
I HEARD A BIRD SING

DAY / YEAR	DAY / WEEK	DAY / MONTH	SUN RISE	SUN SET	LENGTH OF DAY	TIDE AM	TIDE PM	MOON	ON THIS DAY
351	Mon	17	7:19	4:53	10/34	6:02H	12:05L 5:46H 11:41L	◑	1602: Sebastian Vizcaino lands at Monterey Bay, and the country taken in the name of the King of Spain.
352	Tues	18	7:20	4:53	10/33	6:44H	1:15L 7:22H	◖	1883: Landowners are warned that the Sacramento River is being diverted for for irrigation.
353	Wed	19	7:20	4:53	10/33	12:34L 7:28H	2:19L 8:52H	◖	1910: Edward Douglass White is sworn in as the ninth Chief Justice of the U.S.
354	Thurs	20	7:21	4:54	10/33	1:29L 8:13H	3:16L 10:09H	◖	1941: The *SS Emidio* is attacked by the Imperial Japanese Navy north of San Francisco.
355	Fri	21	7:21	4:54	10/33	2:27L 9:01H	4:10L 11:13H	(	1937: Disney's *Snow White and the Seven Dwarfs* premieres.
356	Sat	22	7:22	4:55	10/33	3:24L 9:50H	5:01L	○	2003: An earthquake strikes near San Simeon, registering a 6.5 magnitude.
357	Sun	23	7:22	4:55	10/33	12:09H 4:20L 10:40H	5:50L	○	2003: Gov. Arnold Schwarzenegger declares a state of emergency in San Luis Obispo County, following the San Simeon earthquake.
358	Mon	24	7:23	4:56	10/33	12:49H 5:14L 11:30H	6:37L	○	1849: A fire that breaks out at Dennison's Exchange on the east side of Kearny between Clay and Jackson streets destroys most of the city.
359	Tues	25	7:23	4:57	10/34	1:46H 6:08L	12:19H 7:23L	○	1868: Pres. Andrew Johnson grants unconditional pardon to all Civil War Confederate soldiers.
360	Wed	26	7:24	4:57	10/33	2:31H 7:02L	1:08H 8:06L	)	1873: Tiburcio Vásquez and his bandit gang rob the village of Kingston.
361	Thurs	27	7:24	4:58	10/34	3:15H 7:58L	1:58H 8:48L	)	1947: The children's television program *Howdy Doody* makes its debut on NBC.
362	Fri	28	7:24	4:58	10/34	3:58H 8:50L	2:50H 9:29L	)	1836: Spain recognizes independence of Mexico.
363	Sat	29	7:24	4:59	10/35	4:40H 10:02L	3:47H 10:10L	◗	2003: Homeland Security institutes armed security on flights when it believes there is a threat.
364	Sun	30	7:25	5:00	10/35	5:22H 11:11L	4:55H 10:51L	◗	1975: Golfer Eldrick "Tiger" Woods is born in Cypress.
365	Mon	31	7:25	5:01	10/36	6:03H	12:21L 6:21L 11:31L	◑	1849: Population of San Francisco is estimated at 100,000.

● NEW MOON   ◖ FIRST QUARTER   ○ FULL MOON   ◗ LAST QUARTER

EARTH QUAKE!

BIG MYTHS ABOUT THE BIG ONE

1) Animals can predict, or sense, earthquakes.
Who knows if Spot's erratic behavior is due to an impending temblor or the cat across the street? Sure, changes in animal behavior have sometimes been observed prior to earthquakes, but not consistently.

2) Earthquakes always happen in the early morning.
This is a persistent myth, even though we know that earthquakes can't tell time! For example, the 1992 Joshua Tree earthquake was at 9:50 p.m., the 1940 Imperial Valley event was at 8:37 p.m., and the 1989 Loma Prieta quake at 5:02 p.m.

3) Hot and dry—it's earthquake weather!
This myth dates to the ancient Greeks, who authored quite a few myths. But the fact is, no scientific correlation with weather has been found.

4) The earth will split wide open.
This one only exists in the movies, where it makes for some spectacular special effects. Thing is, if the fault could open, there would be no friction, and without friction, there would be no earthquake. Post-earthquake settling can open fissures and create drop-offs, though. Uh-oh.

5) Little earthquakes keep big ones from happening.
While a small quake may ease stress on a fault line temporarily, it doesn't prevent larger ones, which has to do with the amount of energy released.

6) Earthquakes are becoming more frequent.

It just seems as if there are more because we have better equipment to locate earthquakes that would have gone undetected before. Actual research shows that earthquakes of magnitude 7.0 or greater have remained fairly constant throughout the century—and have actually decreased in recent years.

7) California's gonna fall into the sea.

Those folks in Arizona just envy our beachfront property! But seriously, the San Andreas Fault System is the dividing line between two tectonic plates, and they're moving horizontally, not vertically. Landslides and other changes dues to earthquake activity could change the shape of the coastline, though.

8) Head for the doorway.

This is a great idea—if you live in an old, unreinforced adobe house. In today's homes the doorway is no stronger than any other part of the house, and you could be hurt by the swinging door. Get under a table!

Pack Your Snowsuit!

Q: I want to move out of the earthquake zone; where can I go?

A: Earthquakes can happen anywhere, but the continent of Antarctica has the least number of earthquakes than anywhere else in the world.

What, Me Worry?

Not every building in California was built before earthquakes codes were in place, so it's best to be prepared. Stash an earthquake kit (food, water, flashlight, etc.), and develop a plan with your family (how to exit the house, where to meet, etc.). Here is what you should do during an earthquake:

- If you're inside, stay there. Get under a sturdy table or desk and hang on to it.
- Get out of the kitchen.
- Do not run outside.
- If you are outside, get into the open, away from power lines and anything that might fall on you.
- If you are driving, stop carefully, away from anything that might fall on you. Remain in your car until the shaking stops.
- If you are on or near a steep hillside, watch for landslides.
- If you are on the coast, drop, cover, and hold on until

A WHOLE LOTTA SHAKIN' GOIN' ON

Californians have been paying attention to earthquakes since the beginning of time, but they've only been documenting them since the early nineteenth century, and then not always reliably. (The first documented earthquake in California happened July 28, 1769, experienced by Spanish missionaries near Los Angeles.)

A rough count of reported earthquakes measuring 5.0 or higher between 1800 and 2000 yields 226 temblors ... and there are dozens of smaller ones happening every day. (How many, you ask? Visit quake.usgs.gov/recenteqs/ to see a map showing quakes that have happened in the last hour/day/week. It may surprise you.)

Here are some of the memorable ones:

YEAR	DAY	TIME	LOCATION/NAME	RICHTER	REGION
1812	Dec. 8	7:00a	San Juan Capistrano	7.0	South
1857	Jan. 9	8:00a	Fort Tejon	8.25	South
1868	Oct. 21	7:53a	Hayward	7.0	North
1872	Mar. 26	2:30a	Owens Valley/Lone Pine	7.6	South
1906	Apr. 18	5:12a	San Francisco	8.25	North
1918	Apr. 21	4:32p	San Jacinto	6.9	South
1940	May 18	8:36p	Imperial Valley	7.1	South
1952	Jul. 20	3:52a	Kern County	7.7	South
1971	Feb. 9	6:00a	San Fernando	6.7	South
1979	Oct. 15	3:17p	Imperial Valley	6.4	South
1980	Nov. 8	2:27a	Gorda Plate	7.2	North
1983	May 2	3:42p	Coalinga	6.7	Central
1989	Oct. 17	5:04p	Loma Prieta	7.1	North
1992	Apr. 25	10:06a	Cape Mendocino	7.2	North
1992	Jun. 28	3:57a	Landers/Big Bear	7.3	South
1994	Jan. 17	4:30a	Northridge	6.7	South
1999	Oct. 16	2:45a	Hector Mine	7.0	South

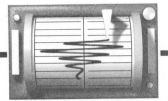

HOW BIG WAS IT?

Here's an interesting little chart to give you an idea of just exactly how much damage one of these babies can do:

RICHTER SCALE	EXAMPLE	TNT EQUIVALENT
0.5	Hand grenade	6 lb.
1.0	Construction site blast	30 lb.
1.5	WWII conventional bombs	320 lb.
2.0	Late WWII conventional bombs	1 metric ton
2.5	WWII blockbuster bomb	4.6 metric tons
3.0	Massive Ordnance Air Blast (MOAB) bomb	29 metric tons
3.5	Chelyabinsk USSR nuclear accident, 1957	73 metric tons
4.0	Small atomic bomb	1 kiloton
4.5	Average tornado (total energy)	5.1 kiloton
5.0	Nagasaki atomic bomb	32 kiloton
5.5	Sierra Madre quake, 1991	80 kiloton
6.0	Parkfield quake, 2004	1 megaton
6.5	Northridge quake, 1994	approx. 5 megatons
7.0	Largest thermonuclear weapon	approx. 50 megatons
7.5	Landers quake, 1992	approx. 160 megatons
8.0	San Francisco quake, 1906	approx. 1 gigaton
8.5	Anchorage (AK) quake, 1964	approx. 5 gigaton
9.0	2004 Indian Ocean earthquake	approx. 30 gigaton

Source: Wikipedia (Richter Magnitude Scale)

The Richter Magnitude Scale was developed in 1935 by a scientist working at Caltech, Charles Richter. It is not used to express damage, only amplitude. Each whole number increase in magnitude represents the release of about 31 times more energy than the preceding whole number.

World's LARGEST Thermometer

It makes sense that the world's largest thermometer is located near the spot that routinely sets records for heat. We're talking about Death Valley, of course, which in 1913 posted an official temperature of 134° F.

So when Will Herron (then-owner of the next-door Bun Boy restaurant) decided to build the world's largest thermometer in Baker, it had to be 134 feet tall. Baker's located in the Mojave Desert at the junction of Interstate 15 and Highway 127, and bills itself as the Gateway to Death Valley. The town's 914 residents work in the seven gas stations, ten fast-food chains, five restaurants, and three motels that service the tourists traveling between Los Angeles and Las Vegas.

Erected in 1991, the thermometer cost $700,000, used 33 tons of steel, and required almost 5,000 neon lamps—and was soon destroyed by gusty desert winds. Rebuilt (and filled with concrete this time!) the Baker thermometer is now a notable tourist attraction in its own right (it's located at 72155 Baker Boulevard) and can be seen for miles away!

How Hot Was It?

- Highest temperature recorded / 134 F, Death Valley / Jul. 10, 1913*
- Lowest temperature recorded / -45 F, Boca / Jan. 20, 1937
- Highest wind velocity / 101 mph gust, Sandberg / Mar, 25, 1975
- Record snow depth on ground / 451 in., Tamarack / Mar. 11, 1911
- Record 24-hour snowfall / 67.0 in., Echo Summit / Jan. 4–5, 1982
- Record 1-month snowfall / 390 in., Tamarack / Jan. 1911
- Least 1-season rainfall / 0.00 in., Death Valley / 1929
- Record 1-hour rainfall / 4.7 in., Mt. Palomar / Aug. 13, 1992
- Record 24-hour rainfall / 26.12 in., Hoegees Camp / Jan. 22–23, 1943
- Record 1-year rainfall / 153.54 in., Monumental / 1909

* also the official highest temperature in the Western Hemisphere and the second hottest in the world

Santa Anas or Santanas?

Californians are of two minds about the nomenclature of those hot, dry winds that blow westward onto Southern California, often bringing wildfires with them. The meteorological term is föhn wind—a wind that is forced, under pressure, over a mountain range, then drains off on the downslope, gathering speed as it goes. (It's a popular misconception that the Santa Ana wind is hot because it starts in the Mojave and Sonoran Deserts. Although that's true, the winds occur in fall and early spring, when temperatures in the high desert are relatively cool. It's the high pressure that does it.)

Are they the Santa Ana winds because of the Santa Ana Mountains west of Los Angeles? Or is the name really Santanas (devil winds)? It doesn't matter—Southern Californians dread them, as they can raise temperatures as much as 50°F in a matter of hours.

There was a desert wind blowing that night.

It was one of those hot, dry Santa Anas that come down through the mountain passes and curl your hair and make your nerves jump and your skin itch.

On nights like that every booze party ends in a fight. Meek little wives feel the edge of the carving knife and study their husbands' necks. Anything can happen.

—RAYMOND CHANDLER, *"RED WIND"* (1938)

PaLM SPRiNGS PLaYGROUND

Once a trendy getaway for the Hollywood elite, the twenty-first century Palm Springs is still chic and charming. Here are a few fun facts about this desert city:

- Permanent, year-round population is 43,800; an additional snowbird population boosts winter numbers to 75,000.
- Approximately 1.6 million people vacation in Palm Springs each year.
- Sunny days number at least 350 per year.
- Average temperature in January: 70° F; average July temperature: 108° F.
- More than 41 percent of the population is over 65.
- While enjoying a swim in a backyard pool, Palm Springs residents can see the snow-capped Mt. Jacinto.
- Visitors riding the tramcars to the top of Mt. Jacinto (about 15 minutes) will experience an approximate 30-degree drop in temperature.
- All of the performers of the acclaimed Palm Springs Follies vaudeville show are over the age of 55.
- Palm Springs hosts several world-class annual sporting events including the largest LPGA tournament, the Bob Hope Chrysler Classic (usually the first PGA event of the season), and a major tennis tournament.

LAVA LAND

Apart from its history as a once-famous stop on Route 66—with the fifties-era Roy's Motel and Café a familiar sight—Amboy (located about sixty miles northeast of Twentynine Palms) is the location of Amboy Crater.

An extinct cinder cone volcano, the crater is between six and ten thousand years old, and is surrounded by lava flows that are just as old. Use the west trail from the parking area and hike up about 250 feet to have a look at the crater of this National Historic Landmark, a souvenir of California's ancient history!

THE MYSTERY OF THE LITTLE BOY

The phenomenon we call El Niño is a naturally occurring two-to-seven-year cycle of changes in the ocean-atmosphere system. In normal years, the Pacific Ocean is warmer on its western side and cooler near the Americas. In El Niño years, that warm water shifts eastward, the westward-moving trade winds slow to a crawl—and the results of this shift cause significant weather and climate events literally around the globe. It starts on the Pacific coasts of North and South America.

The shift of the warm water and the change in the wind patterns are linked, but scientists don't yet know which is the cause and which the effect. In other words: it's a mystery.

What we do know is what happens: the warm ocean feeds thunderstorms above, creating increased rainfall, flash flooding, and mudslides along the coasts of Peru, Chile, Mexico, and California. Drier conditions on the other side of the Pacific increase forest fires in the Philippines and Australia. Winters are milder in the upper Midwest and Canada in an El Niño year. The fishing industry is also affected.

You can't put Mother Nature into a computer, but today, using satellite observation data, computer models, and other data, scientists are learning to predict—and someday solve—the mystery of El Niño.

And La Niña?
It's the opposite of El Niño—ocean temperatures on the eastern side of the Pacific are cooler than normal.

EL NIÑO 1982–83

Ask any scientist for a list of weather disasters, and the El Niño episode of 1982–83 will end up on it. Thanks to late twentieth-century technology, it's also the strongest event to ever come under scientific scrutiny. Here's a worldwide snapshot of that season:

- El Niño conditions produced widespread famine in Indonesia in 1983.
- Bush fires arising from droughts in South Australia and Victoria resulted in the loss of 75 lives and more than 2,000 houses.
- The anchovy fishing industry off the coast of Peru was destroyed due to lack of fish.
- Floods devastated the coasts of both South and North America.
- Torrential rains and severe storms pounded southern China.
- Forest fires erupted in parts of Southeast Asia and Brazil, destroying valuable rainforest.
- Indonesia experienced the worst drought of the previous 50 years.
- Guadalajara, Mexico, saw snow for the first time since 1881.
- Nearly all of the fur seal pups in the Galapagos Islands chain were lost due to lack of food.
- More than 17 million birds in the Christmas Islands died of starvation, dooming their recently hatched young.
- Albatross, cormorants, penguins, and marine iguanas populations were also adversely affected by the lack of food.

- Flooding on the Korean Peninsula claimed 180 lives and drove 90,000 people from their homes.
- Peru recorded its greatest rainfall amounts in more than 200 years.
- Guayaquil, Ecuador, recorded 13 times its normal rainfall during the El Niño period.
- Torrential rains also produced a continuous heavy surf that resulted in widespread coastal damage to Peru and Ecuador; damage was estimated at $650 billion.
- Overflowing rivers such as the Piura in Peru wiped out prime banana- and rice-growing regions.
- Unsanitary conditions caused by flood damage resulted in virulent diseases spreading throughout the flooded area in South America.
- El Niño 1982–83 led to the death of some 2000 people worldwide and caused losses amounting to approximately $12 billion.
- In California, repeated severe storms brought high wind, heavy rain, and heavy snowfall; this resulted in wind damage, higher tides, flash floods in coastal and valley locations, mudslides in coastal mountain areas, record snowfall in the Sierra Mountains, and flooding during the spring snowmelt. Forty-six counties were declared disaster areas.
- Damage in California: 36 dead, 481 injured, $1.209 billion economic losses including 6,661 homes and 1,330 businesses.

Wherefore Art Thou, Niño?

In 1983, a triggerfish was spotted in water off the Alaskan coastline. A tropical fish normally found in the Indo-Pacific, the sighting placed this fish more than 1,700 miles farther north than any other triggerfish had been sighted! It must have followed the warm currents fed by El Niño ... where it ended up in arctic waters.

A tropical triggerfish.

BEYOND THE WEEKEND WARRIOR

PROFESSIONAL SPORTS IN CALIFORNIA

NATIONAL FOOTBALL LEAGUE

- Oakland Raiders / McAfee Coliseum
- San Francisco 49ers / Monster Park (formerly Candlestick Park)
- San Diego Chargers / Qualcomm Stadium

NATIONAL BASKETBALL ASSOCIATION

- Golden State Warriors (Oakland) / The Arena in Oakland
- Los Angeles Lakers / Staples Center
- Los Angeles Clippers / Staples Center
- Sacramento Kings / ARCO Arena II

MAJOR LEAGUE BASEBALL

- Los Angeles Angels (Anaheim) / Angel Stadium
- Los Angeles Dodgers / Dodger Stadium
- Oakland Athletics / McAfee Coliseum
- San Diego Padres / PETCO Park
- San Francisco Giants / AT&T Park

NATIONAL HOCKEY LEAGUE

- Anaheim Ducks / Arrowhead Pond of Anaheim
- Los Angeles Kings / Staples Center
- San Jose Sharks / HP Pavilion at San Jose

MAJOR LEAGUE SOCCER

- Club Deportivo Chivas USA (Carson) / Home Depot Center
- Los Angeles Galaxy (Carson) / The Home Depot Center

Soccer Scores
The Los Angeles Galaxy has the highest all-time attendance in MLS league history and is the first team in the league to make a profit in a season. Notable players include Landon Donovan, Cobi Jones, and Chris Albright.

GROWING PLAYERS

When the minor league baseball league system was formed in the 1930s, major league players often joked that they were "growing players down on the farm like corn." They've been called "farm teams" ever since!

- Bakersfield Blaze (Texas Rangers)
- High Desert (Adelanto) Mavericks (Kansas City Royals)
- Inland Empire 66ers (San Bernardino) (Seattle Mariners)
- Lake Elsinore Storm (San Diego Padres)
- Lancaster JetHawks (Arizona Diamondbacks)
- Modesto Nuts (Colorado Rockies)
- Rancho Cucamonga Quakes (Los Angeles Angels)
- San Jose Giants (San Francisco Giants)
- Stockton Ports (Oakland Athletics)
- Visalia Oaks (Tampa Bay Devil Rays)

Take Me Out to the Ball Game

The San Jose Giants pride themselves on playing great baseball and providing an old-fashioned baseball experience for the fans, including plenty of promotions and fan games. One very popular feature is the Beer Batter. A player from the opposing team is designated the Beer Batter, and if the San Jose pitcher strikes him out, beer is half price for fifteen minutes immediately following the strike out!

Casey at the Bat

Baseball in Stockton goes 'way back ... to the 1860s. An 1880s team, forerunner of the current, much-loved Ports, is thought to have been the inspiration for Ernest Thayer's well-known poem. Thayer was a journalist for the San Francisco Examiner at the time, while the Stockton team's games were played in a ballpark on Banner Island...a place once known as Mudville.

THE STICK

It may say "Monster Park" on the signs outside, but to locals this stadium is and will always be Candlestick Park. In fact, a proposition passed in the 2004 election ensures that the name will revert permanently to Candlestick when the Monster contract expires in 2008.

Built in 1958 on a spit of land (Candlestick Point) perched on the San Francisco Bay, the Stick was home to baseball's San Francisco Giants until 2000. In 1971 they were joined by the NFL's San Francisco 49ers, who play there still.

As a baseball stadium, Candlestick Park was plagued by windy conditions that made life difficult for outfielders and batters alike. In 1963, a gust picked up the batting cage and dropped it on the pitcher's mound—sixty feet away! And that wasn't the only threat to ball fans: in October 1989 the Loma Prieta earthquake (7.1 on the Richter Scale) delayed Game 3 of the World Series for ten days.

A Hard Day's Night
The Beatles' last live concert was at Candlestick Park on August 29, 1966. They played for 33 minutes to 24,000 screaming fans.

Stargazing at Lakers' Games

The Los Angeles Lakers' home games routinely sport any number of celebrities in near-court seats—and some of them are diehard fans! Denzel Washington, Leonardo DiCaprio, Edward Norton, Andy Garcia, Dyan Cannon, members of the rock group Red Hot Chili Peppers, and, of course, Jack Nicholson, are spotted regularly at Staples Arena. Jack has been a Lakers season ticket holder since 1967.

NCAA DIVISION 1 FOOTBALL IN CALIFORNIA

SCHOOL	TEAM	FOUNDED	ENROLLMENT	LOCATION
California State University–Fresno	Bulldogs	1911	21,000	Fresno
San Diego State University	Aztecs	1897	33,676	San Diego
San Jose State University	Spartans	1862	28,932	San Jose
Stanford Univ.	Cardinals	1891	14,654	Palo Alto
University of California–Berkeley	Golden Bears	1868	33,000	Berkeley
Univ. of California –Los Angeles	Bruins	1919	38,000	Los Angeles
University of Southern California	Trojans	1880	32,160	Los Angeles

NCAA DIVISION 1 BASKETBALL IN CALIFORNIA

Note: all teams listed on the NCAA Division 1 football list also field basketball teams; this list includes NCAA Division 1 schools that do not field football teams.

SCHOOL	TEAM	FOUNDED	ENROLLMENT	LOCATION
California Polytechnic State University	Broncos	1901	17,683	San Luis Obispo
California State University–Fullerton	Titans	1957	35,040	Fullerton
California State University–Northridge	Matadors	1958	33,000	Northridge
Long Beach State University	49ers	1949	39,863	Long Beach
Loyola Marymount University	Lions	1865	7,104	Los Angeles
Pepperdine University	Waves	1937	6,053	Malibu
St. Mary's College of California	Gaels	1863	4,536	Moraga
Santa Clara University	Broncos	1851	8,047	Santa Clara
University of the Pacific	Tigers	1861	6,268	Stockton
University of California–Irvine	Anteaters	1965	24,362	Irvine
University of California–Riverside	Highlanders	1907	16,622	Riverside
University of California–Santa Barbara	Gauchos	1944	20,559	Santa Barbara
University of San Diego	Toreros	1949	6,452	San Diego
University of San Francisco	Dons	1855	7,487	San Francisco

CALIFORNIANS IN THE FOOTBALL HALL OF FAME

NAME	INDUCTED	BIRTHPLACE	TYPE
Troy Aikman	2006	Covina	player
Marcus Allen	2003	San Diego	player
Dan Fouts	1993	San Francisco	player
Frank Gifford	1997	Santa Monica	player
Mel Hein	1963	Redding	player
James Lofton	2003	Ft. Ord	player
Hugh McElhenny	1970	Los Angeles	player
Ron Mix	1979	Los Angeles	player
Warren Moon	2006	Los Angeles	player
Anthony Muñoz	1998	Ontario	player
Pete Rozelle	1985	South Gate	commissioner
Bob St. Clair	1990	San Francisco	player
Tex Schramm	1991	San Gabriel	administrator
O. J. Simpson	1985	San Francisco	player
Bill Walsh	1993	Los Angeles	coach

Troy Aikman could have played baseball: he was drafted by the New York Mets right out of high school! Instead, he chose to go on to college ... and play a little football.

I Left My Heart in San Francisco

Bob St. Clair was born in San Francisco, grew up there, went to Polytechnic High School, and then to the University of San Francisco, where he was part of USF's undefeated 1951 team. In 1953 he was drafted by the 49ers and played his entire professional career with that team, in the team's then-home, Kezar Stadium—one of the few players in history to do so. The city renamed Kezar's field as a tribute to St. Clair in 2001.

The War of the Roses

Note: the 1942 Rose Bowl Game was played in Durham, NC,
for security reasons, following the attack on Pearl Harbor.

YEAR	WINNING TEAM	LOSING TEAM
1902*	Michigan 49	Stanford 0
1916	Washington State 14	Brown 0
1917	Oregon 14	Pennsylvania 0
1918	Mare Island (USMC) 19	Camp Lewis (US Army) 7
1919	Great Lakes (US Navy) 17	Mare Island 0
1920	Harvard 7	Oregon 6
1921	California 28	Ohio State 0
1922	California 0	Washington & Jefferson 0
1923	Southern California 14	Penn State 3
1924	Washington 14	Navy 14
1925	Notre Dame 27	Stanford 10
1926	Alabama 20	Washington 19
1927	Stanford 7	Alabama 7
1928	Stanford 7	Pittsburgh 6
1929	Georgia Tech 8	California 7
1930	Southern California 47	Pittsburgh 14
1931	Alabama 24	Washington State 0
1932	Southern California 21	Tulane 12
1933	Southern California 35	Pittsburgh 0
1934	Columbia 7	Stanford 0
1935	Alabama 29	Stanford 13
1936	Stanford 7	SMU 0
1937	Pittsburgh 21	Washington 0
1938	California 13	Alabama 0
1939	Southern California 7	Duke 3
1940	Southern California 14	Tennessee 0
1941	Stanford 21	Nebraska 13
1942	Oregon State 20	Duke 16
1943	Georgia 9	UCLA 0
1944	Southern California 29	Washington 0
1945	Southern California 25	Tennessee 0
1946	Alabama 34	Southern California 14
1947	Illinois 45	UCLA 14
1948	Michigan 49	Southern California 0
1949	Northwestern 20	California 14
1950	Ohio State 17	California 14
1951	Michigan 14	California 6
1952	Illinois 40	Stanford 7
1953	Southern California 7	Wisconsin 0
1954	Michigan State 28	UCLA 20
1955	Ohio State 20	Southern California 7
1956	Michigan State 17	UCLA 14
1957	Iowa 35	Oregon State 19

First game was a one-off.

Rose Bowl Games, cont.

1958	Ohio State 10	Oregon 7
1959	Iowa 38	California 12
1960	Washington 44	Wisconsin 8
1961	Washington 17	Minnesota 7
1962	Minnesota 21	UCLA 3
1963	Southern California 42	Wisconsin 37
1964	Illinois 17	Washington 7
1965	Michigan 34	Oregon State 7
1966	UCLA 14	Michigan State 12
1967	Purdue 14	Southern California 13
1968	Southern California 14	Indiana 3
1969	Ohio State 27	Southern California 16
1970	Southern California 10	Michigan 3
1971	Stanford 27	Ohio State 17
1972	Stanford 13	Michigan 12
1973	Southern California 42	Ohio State 17
1974	Ohio State 42	Southern California 21
1975	Southern California 18	Ohio State 17
1976	UCLA 23	Ohio State 10
1977	Southern California 14	Michigan 6
1978	Washington 27	Michigan 20
1979	Southern California 17	Michigan 10
1980	Southern California 17	Ohio State 16
1981	Michigan 23	Washington 6
1982	Washington 28	Iowa 0
1983	UCLA 24	Michigan 14
1984	UCLA 45	Illinois 9
1985	Southern California 20	Ohio State 17
1986	UCLA 45	Iowa 28
1987	Arizona State 22	Michigan 15
1988	Michigan State 20	Southern California 17
1989	Michigan 22	Southern California 14
1990	Southern California 17	Michigan 10
1991	Washington 46	Iowa 34
1992	Washington 34	Michigan 14
1993	Michigan 38	Washington 31
1994	Wisconsin 21	UCLA 16
1995	Penn State 38	Oregon 20
1996	Southern California 41	Northwestern 32
1997	Ohio State 20	Arizona State 17
1998	Michigan 21	Washington State 16
1999	Wisconsin 38	UCLA 31
2000	Wisconsin 17	Stanford 9
2001	Washington 34	Purdue 24
2002	Miami (FL) 37	Nebraska 14
2003	Oklahoma 34	Washington State 14
2004	Southern California 28	Michigan 14
2005	Texas 38	Michigan 37
2006	Texas 41	Southern California 38

He DiD It His Wave...

One of the more amusing controversies in sports is the competing claims of who invented the Wave—the stadium phenomenon in which groups of fans stand and sit rapidly in succession, causing a wavelike motion when viewed from a distance. Like, say, on national television.

Self-named Californian Krazy George Henderson has just that. It was October 15, 1981, and Henderson, a professional cheerleader, had been waiting for the right circumstances: a packed stadium and an excited crowd. The American League championship playoff game between the Oakland A's and New York Yankees at the Oakland Coliseum was just such a game, and there it is, folks, on videotape. It was so unusual and unexpected that the cameramen definitely caught it, and people who were there, like Joe Garagiola, former NBC sports commentator who called the game that day, have discussed what they saw for the record.

None of this was in dispute until 2000, when a few University of Washington Huskies fans saw (www.krazygeorge.com—what else?) Krazy George's Web site and begged to differ. It seems that the Huskies have declared that one of their cheerleaders invented the Wave back in 1981 too. It says so on their Web site. And Huskies fans have demanded Krazy George stop saying he invented the fan participation move event that happens now in stadiums all over the world.

For the record, the Huskies claim to have invented the Wave on October 31, 1981. Since that's more than two weeks after the nationally televised A's/Yankees game, we consider this case closed.

World's First Professional Cheerleader

Krazy George Henderson was a student at San Jose State University in 1968 when he started cheering at football games—just for fun, then later on the cheerleading squad. After graduation, Henderson became a high school teacher, but he continued to cheer at Bay Area games for free, gaining no small amount of notoriety. By 1975 he'd been hired by local minor league teams to cheer, and that same year was hired to do just one game for the Kansas City Chiefs—which turned into a permanent gig. He's been cheering professionally ever since.

Baseball Hall of Famers Born in California

NAME	BIRTHPLACE	INDUCTED	POSITION
Gary Carter	Culver City	2003	player
Frank Chance	Fresno	1946	player
Joe Cronin	San Francisco	1956	player
Joe DiMaggio	Martinez	1955	player
Bobby Doerr	Los Angeles	1986	player
Don Drysdale	Van Nuys	1984	player
Dennis Eckersley	Oakland	2004	player
Vernon "Lefty" Gomez	Rodeo	1972	player
Charles "Chick" Hafey	Berkeley	1971	player
Harry Heilmann	San Francisco	1952	player
Harry Hooper	Bell Station	1971	player
George Kelly	San Francisco	1973	player
Tony Lazzeri	San Francisco	1991	player
Bob Lemon	San Bernardino	1976	player
Ernie Lombardi	Oakland	1986	player
Eddie Murray	Los Angeles	2003	player
Tom Seaver	Fresno	1992	player
Duke Snider	Los Angeles	1980	player
Ted Williams	San Diego	1966	player

JOLtiN' JOE

The eighth of an Italian fisherman's nine children, San Francisco's favorite son, Joe DiMaggio, played his entire professional career for the New York Yankees. In his thirteen-year career with the Yankees, DiMaggio amassed an amazing set of statistics (including that fifty-six-consecutive-game hitting streak in 1941) and is one of the game's all-time greats. Pundits note that DiMaggio's numbers—notably his home runs—would likely have been better in any other stadium in the nation: left-center field in Yankee Stadium went back to 475 feet (compared to ballparks today where left-center rarely reaches 380 feet). Hits that would have been home runs anywhere else were just long outs there.

Tinkers to Evers to Chance

Playing baseball in an era when fantastic sports plays were immortalized in poetry rather than in fifteen-second video clips on weekend highlights reels, Fresno native and first baseman Frank Chance (1877–1924) is best known now for his mention in a 1910 poem about his famous double plays:

BASEBALL'S SAD LEXICON

These are the saddest of possible words:
Tinker to Evers to Chance.
Trio of Bear-cubs, fleeter than birds,
Tinker to Evers to Chance.
Ruthlessly pricking our gonfalon bubble,
Making a Giant hit into a double—
Words that are weighty with nothing but trouble:
Tinker to Evers to Chance.

—FRANKLIN P. ADAMS,
published in the *New York Evening Mail*

[Tom Seaver] is so good that blind people come to the park just to hear him pitch.
—REGGIE JACKSON
(1946–)

If You Film It They Will Come

Bang the Drum Slowly / 1973 / Robert De Niro

Bull Durham / 1988 / Kevin Costner, Susan Sarandon

Cobb / 1994 / Tommy Lee Jones

Eight Men Out / 1988 / John Cusack, David Straithairn

Field of Dreams / 1989 / Kevin Costner

A League of Their Own / 1992 / Tom Hanks, Geena Davis

The Natural / 1984 / Robert Redford, Robert Duvall

Pride of the Yankees / 1942 / Gary Cooper

The Sandlot / 1993 / Tom Guiry

61* / 2001 / Barry Pepper, Thomas Jane

The Voice of the Lakers

Chick Hearn (1916–2002) set the standard for calling professional basketball games (even in the television era, the Lakers preferred to simulcast his broadcasts to radio, after most teams switched to using different announcers). He was enshrined in the Basketball Hall of Fame as a contributor in 2003.

Earning the spot as the Los Angeles Lakers' play-by-play announcer in 1961, Hearn broadcast 3,338 consecutive Lakers games, a streak that started on November 21, 1965. (The previous evening he'd been stranded in Fayetteville, Arkansas, by bad weather, only the second game he'd ever missed.)

Hearn's lasting contributions to the game, however, are what fans call "Chick-isms": a vast lexicon of colorful descriptions such as slam-dunk, air ball, give-and-go, dribble drive, no-look pass, and many more. Slam-dunk seems like a phrase as old as basketball, but in fact Los Angeles fans heard it first.

This beloved play-by-play announcer's string of consecutive games came to an end during the 2001–02 season when he underwent heart surgery. On recovery, Hearn returned to work, and eventually called Game 4 of the NBA Finals, when the Lakers defeated the New Jersey Nets. He died later that summer, but lives on in the hearts of Lakers fans.

FiRSt COUPLe OF SPORt

Basketball Hall of Famer Ann Meyers was an amazing sportswoman. The first player to be part of the U.S. national team while still in high school (a team that went on to win the silver medal at the 1976 Olympic Games), she was also the first woman to be signed to a four-year athletic college scholarship (UCLA). Upon her graduation she held twelve of thirteen school records. Meyers went on to be the first woman to sign a contract with a National Basketball Association team, the Indiana Pacers.

As if this weren't enough, Ann Meyers married former Los Angeles Dodger Baseball Hall of Fame pitcher Don Drysdale, making them the first married couple who were members of their respective sports' Halls of Fame.

CHICK-ISMS

Air-ball: a shot that doesn't even get close

Boo birds: fans that boo their own team when the Lakers are doing badly

Building a house: what a player who is throwing bricks is doing

Bunny hop in the pea patch: traveling

Call it with Braille: a blatant foul that will be easy for the official to call

Charity stripe: free-throw line

Finger roll: a shot that rolls off the shooter's fingers

Garbage time: sloppily played remainder of the game (after it's in the refrigerator)

Give-and-go: Player passes, moves, and gets a return pass

Good Lord and four disciples couldn't beat the Lakers tonight: the Lakers are playing really well

He's human after all: a player's been on a shooting streak and finally misses

He's not a happy camper: the official made a call that the player doesn't like

If that goes in I'm walking home: (usually said on the road) hopeless pass

It's in the refrigerator: we know the winner, only the final score is in question (also: "It's in the refrigerator, the door is closed, the light is out, the eggs are cooling, the butter's getting hard and the Jell-O's jigglin'"!)

Matador defense: bad defense; the lane opens up like a matador pulling his cape away

Mustard's off the hot dog: a show-off play results in a turnover (or is unsuccessful)

No harm, no foul (no blood, no ambulance): contact occurs but official doesn't call

Not Phi Beta Kappa: not a particularly smart play

On him like a postage stamp: a very tight defense

Picked his pocket: a steal so fast the victim didn't even see it happen

(They couldn't beat) Sisters of Mercy: the Lakers are playing badly tonight

Slaaaam dunk: called when the ball's been dunked

Throws up a brick: a player makes an errant shot

Throws up a prayer: a wild shot that needs a miracle to score

---

WOMEN'S NBA TEAMS IN CALIFORNIA

- Los Angeles Sparks (founded 1997)

- Sacramento Monarchs

Basketball Hall of Famers

NAME	BIRTHPLACE	INDUCTED	POSITION
Denny Crum	San Fernando	1994	coach
Gail Goodrich	Los Angeles	1996	player
Alex Hannum	Los Angeles	1998	coach
Lloyd Leith	San Francisco	1983	coach
Angelo "Hank" Luisetti	San Francisco	1959	player
Ann Meyers	San Diego	1993	player
Vern Mikkelsen	Fresno	1995	player
Cheryl Miller	Riverside	1995	player
Jim Pollard	Oakland	1978	player
Bill Walton	La Mesa	1993	player
George Yardley	Hollywood	1996	player

You Go, Guy!

Young Californian Ken Venturi (you know him, perhaps, as an announcer for CBS Sports) made the golf world sit up and pay attention when, as an amateur, he finished second in the 1956 Masters after leading from the first round. Only a final round under difficult conditions prevented him from winning outright and thus becoming the first amateur in the history of the Masters to do so.

San Diego-born Phil Mickelson is ambidextrous: he swings a golf club left-handed, but writes right-handed. He is one of only five golfers ever to have ever shot 59 in competition.

CALIFORNIA GOLF COURSES

on "America's 100 Greatest Golf Courses 2005–06"

RANK	NAME	LOCATION	DESIGNED BY	YEAR
4	Cypress Point Club	Pebble Beach	Alister Mackenzie, Robert Hunter	1928
6	Pebble Beach Golf Links	Pebble Beach	Jack Neville, Douglas Grant	1919
25	The Olympic Club, Lake Course	San Francisco	Sam Whiting	1928
31	San Francisco Golf Club	San Francisco	A. W. Tillinghast	1918
37	Los Angeles Country Club, North Course	Los Angeles	George C. Thomas Jr.	1921
47	Riviera Country Club	Pacific Palisades	George C. Thomas Jr., W. P. Bell	1926
53	Spyglass Hill Golf Course	Pebble Beach	Robert Trent Jones	1966
54	The Quarry at La Quinta	La Quinta	Tom Fazio	1994
67	Mayacama Golf Club	Santa Rosa	Jack Nicklaus	2001
69	Valley Club of Montecito	Santa Barbara	Alister Mackenzie, Robert Hunter	1929
83	The Preserve Golf Club	Carmel	Tom Fazio, J. Michael Poellot, Sandy Tatum	2000

Source: *Golf Digest*, May 2005

PGA Players of the Year from California

NAME	BIRTHPLACE	YEAR
Tiger Woods	Cypress	2005, 1999–2003, 1997
Corey Pavin	Oxnard	1991
John Daley	Carmichael	1991 Rookie of the Year
Johnny Miller	San Francisco	1974
Billy Casper	San Diego	1970
Ken Venturi	San Francisco	1964

Tiger "By the Tail"

Tiger Woods, who grew up in California, is one of the most celebrated athletes in the world, so you may think you've heard it all. But here are a few things we thought were interesting:

• Tiger won the 9–10 boys' event at the Junior World Golf Championships in 1984. . . when he was eight (it was the youngest group available).

• Woods attended Stanford University and while there won the NCAA individual championship; however, he dropped out after two years to attend to his professional golfing career.

• Woods won five U.S. Golf Association Championships before the age of twenty.

• Woods is the only athlete to win *Sports Illustrated's* Sportsman of the Year award twice (in 1996 and 2000).

• He wears a red shirt on the day of the final round, because he believes the color red symbolizes aggression and assertiveness—traits he wants to show up in his golf game that day.

• In 2006, Woods was number two on *Forbes* magazine's "100 Highest Paid Celebrities" list, trailing only Oprah.

Good Guys Finish First

So what does Tiger do with all that money, anyway? Plenty. In addition to buying houses and cars, Woods devotes his time and money to these charitable causes:

• **Tiger Woods Foundation**
  Established in 1996, TWF is all about kids, with golf clinics for the disadvantaged, grant programs, and university scholarships.

• **Target House**
  The TWF supports the Target House at St. Jude Hospital in Memphis, Tennessee, where patients can stay if their child's treatment will be over three months.

• **Start Something**
  This character development program initiated by the TWF is a partnership with Target.

• **In The City Golf Clinics and Festivals**
  Junior golfers get golf lessons and family fun right in their own hometown.

• **Tiger Woods Foundation Youth Clinic**
  Top youth golfers from the In The City program participate in this three-day event at Disney Resorts. TWF also pulls participants from the Make-a-Wish Foundation.

• **Tiger Woods Learning Center**
  This educational facility in Anaheim has a day program for grades 4 to 6 and an after school program for grades 7 to 12, as well as summer and community outreach programs.

• **Target World Challenge**
  Tiger donates his winnings from this charity golf tournament to his foundation.

WHAT IS PEBBLE BEACH?

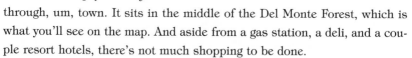

Although there are homes here, and the community post office does have a zip code, Pebble Beach is actually ... a corporation (owned by the Pebble Beach Company). Residents pay homeowners' fees, not city taxes, and the rest of us pay $8.75 just to drive through, um, town. It sits in the middle of the Del Monte Forest, which is what you'll see on the map. And aside from a gas station, a deli, and a couple resort hotels, there's not much shopping to be done.

Of course, there are those golf courses. Eight, to be exact. You've seen a few of them on television, with their astounding views of the ocean:

- Cypress Point Club / 3150 17-Mile Dr. / (831) 624-2223 / private
- Monterey Peninsula Country Club, Dunes Course / 3000 Club Rd. / (831) 373-1556 / private
- Monterey Peninsula Country Club, Shores Course / 3000 Club Rd. / (831) 373-1556 / private
- Pebble Beach Golf Links / 2700 17-Mile Dr. / (831) 625-8518 / public
- Pebble Beach Golf Links, Peter Hay Course / 2700 17-Mile Dr. / (831) 625-8518 / public
- Poppy Hills Golf Course / 3200 Lopez Rd. / (831) 622-8239 / public
- Spanish Bay Golf Links / 2700 17-Mile Dr. / (831) 647-7495 / public
- Spyglass Hill Golf Course / Spyglass Hill Rd. / (831) 625-8563 / public

Two of these award-winning courses (Cypress Point Club and Pebble Beach) rank in the top six of *Golf Digest's* biannual list of the 100 best golf courses in America, and that is no small feat. They are a thrill to play, although they're not inexpensive. But the views of the ocean are unparalleled. And there is that good walk to be had too!

Want to enjoy the panoramic views without concentrating on your golf swing? Splurge on the toll for 17-Mile Drive and enjoy the many scenic overlooks and pullouts you'll find along the way!

FOR A GOOD CAUSE

Charity sporting events are a great time for folks to rub elbows with the stars. Here are some longstanding events that you might enjoy ...

Long Beach Grand Prix Toyota Pro/Celebrity Race

The Long Beach Grand Prix is the premier circuit in the Indy car series, and while plenty of racing fans come out for the main event, others come out the day before the race to watch celebrities and stars compete with professional athletes in a ten-lap thriller that raises money for Racing for Kids.

The St. John's Jimmy Stewart Relay Marathon

Although many charity events are for the "rich and famous," this annual tradition is free and open to the public—and raises half a million dollars for the St. John's Health Center's Child and Family Development Center. With teams fielded by everyone from local firefighters and restaurants (think Spago) to Walt Disney Imagineering and Playboy Playmates, this is a fun family event.

Los Angeles City Annual Police/Celebrity Golf Tournament

For thirty-five years the city of Los Angeles has hosted this golf tournament to raise money for the families of officers killed in the line of duty, and it's gained the support of the entertainment community as well as celebrity golfers. This family-oriented event is open to the public, and includes several LAPD displays of police equipment and skills—and what kid wouldn't be interested in that K-9 squad? Some 10,000 golf fans and autograph-seekers come out each year!

Nautica Malibu Triathlon

For the past twenty years, this charity event has pulled together athletes, celebrities, weekend warriors, and even Special Olympians in a standard three-part race: a half-mile swim in the Pacific, eighteen-mile bicycle race, and a final four-mile race to the finish line. This event benefits the Elizabeth Glaser Pediatric AIDS Foundation.

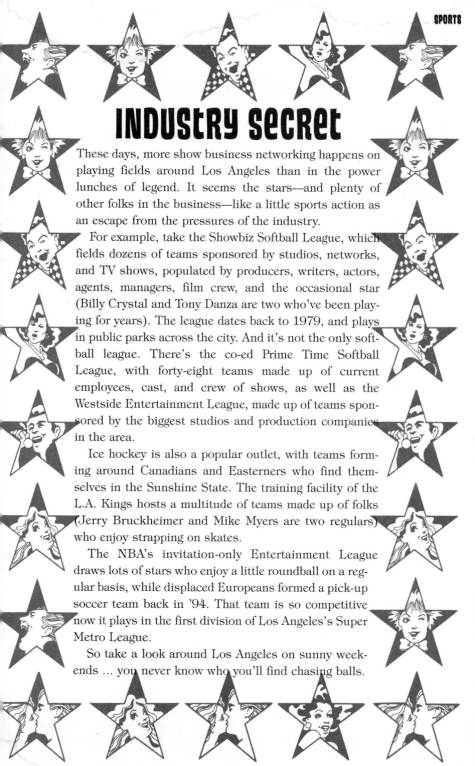

INDUSTRY SECRET

These days, more show business networking happens on playing fields around Los Angeles than in the power lunches of legend. It seems the stars—and plenty of other folks in the business—like a little sports action as an escape from the pressures of the industry.

For example, take the Showbiz Softball League, which fields dozens of teams sponsored by studios, networks, and TV shows, populated by producers, writers, actors, agents, managers, film crew, and the occasional star (Billy Crystal and Tony Danza are two who've been playing for years). The league dates back to 1979, and plays in public parks across the city. And it's not the only softball league. There's the co-ed Prime Time Softball League, with forty-eight teams made up of current employees, cast, and crew of shows, as well as the Westside Entertainment League, made up of teams sponsored by the biggest studios and production companies in the area.

Ice hockey is also a popular outlet, with teams forming around Canadians and Easterners who find themselves in the Sunshine State. The training facility of the L.A. Kings hosts a multitude of teams made up of folks (Jerry Bruckheimer and Mike Myers are two regulars) who enjoy strapping on skates.

The NBA's invitation-only Entertainment League draws lots of stars who enjoy a little roundball on a regular basis, while displaced Europeans formed a pick-up soccer team back in '94. That team is so competitive now it plays in the first division of Los Angeles's Super Metro League.

So take a look around Los Angeles on sunny weekends … you never know who you'll find chasing balls.

130 MILES
130 DEGREES
60 HOURS

Long before the term **extreme sports** was coined in the '90s, a few extreme souls were taking a hike through Death Valley—for, well, if not fun, then for the exhilaration when it's over. The Badwater Ultramarathon is a walk (because, let's face it, you won't be running long in 130-degree heat) from Badwater, the lowest point in the hemisphere, to Whitney Portal, the trailhead for Mount Whitney (the highest point in the hemisphere). Held every year in July, it's been billed as the "World's Toughest Footrace" since 1987. In 2005, there were 81 entrants and 67 official finishers.

Hollywood Turf Club

That's the original name of Hollywood Park. And though it's not located in Hollywood, this landmark thoroughbred racetrack definitely has Hollywood roots. Founded in 1938 as the Hollywood Turf Club, the track was financed by 600 shareholders—the Hollywood elite such as Ralph Bellamy, Joan Blondell, Walt Disney, Bing Crosby, Sam Goldwyn, George Jessel, Al Jolson, and Darryl Zanuck.

HOLLYWOOD PARK TRIVIA

Woolford Farm's Historian traveled by air from Chicago to start in the 1946 Gold Cup, the first time a horse was shipped by air to compete in a specific race.

Citation became horse racing's first million-dollar earner by winning the 1951 Hollywood Gold Cup in his final race.

A trendsetter in giveaway premiums, Hollywood Park attracted a record crowd of 80,348 with a tote bag premium on May 4, 1980.

Wham-O!

The company that brought you (and trademarked) the Frisbee and the Hula Hoop was started in a Los Angeles garage in 1948. When the Hula Hoop was introduced in 1958, Wham-O sold 25 million in two months!

Taste the Sunshine

Those of us who grew up in California's Central Valley often drifted off to sleep as children listening to the gentle swish-swishing sound of irrigation sprinklers. That's because this huge, fertile valley is one of the most productive agricultural regions in the world. A wide, flat valley 400 miles long, the Central Valley was once *in* the Pacific ocean. With the uplift of the coastal ranges millions of years ago, it became an inland sea that eventually filled with sediment from the mountains that surround it, although for millennia the annual snow melt turned the entire valley into one big inland lake. Needless to say, this produced a valley floor of rich, black dirt that will grow virtually anything.

California's largest industry is agriculture (which includes fruit, vegetables, dairy, and wine), and the agribusiness industry is more than twice the size of the state's second industry, aerospace. Agriculture revenue topped $26 billion in 2004.

CALIFORNIA PRODUCES MORE THAN HALF OF THE COUNTRY'S FRUITS, NUTS, AND VEGETABLES. IT IS THE NUMBER-ONE DAIRY STATE, THE NUMBER-TWO COTTON STATE, AND PRODUCES NEARLY 50 PERCENT OF THE NATION'S FLOWERS AND NURSERY PRODUCTS.

Source: California Department of Food and Agriculture

THE MOTHER OF ALL FRUIT STANDS

Take a drive down Highway 152 through the Pacheco Pass near Gilroy and you can't help but notice Casa de Fruta. Founded as an orchard in 1908, the Zanger family opened a roadside cherry stand in 1943. One thing led to another, and now the Zangers' operations include a restaurant, candy store, gas station, playground, and gift shop ... and fabulous California fruit!

PRUNES, PRUNES, GOOD FOR YOUR HEART

Did you know...

- **Avocados** are a popular, profitable crop for California growers, who produce about 90 percent of the American avocado crop (Florida produces just about all of the rest).

- Virtually all the **artichokes** in the U.S. are grown in California, and 75 percent of that crop is produced in Monterey County.

- The U.S. is the world's leading producer of **almonds**, having passed Spain in 1977. Almost all American almond orchards are in California's San Joaquin and Sacramento Valleys.

- **Dates** require particular environmental conditions to produce fruit: a hot, arid climate but plenty of ground water. So dates can only be grown in a few places in the U.S.; 95 percent of the date crop in the U.S. is grown in the Coachella Valley.

- The center of the U.S. **fig**-growing industry is located in Fresno, California, which represents 20 percent of the world production of dried figs.

- **Kiwifruit** cultivation was introduced to California in 1967, and the majority of U.S. production of the fruit is in the Sunshine State.

- California remains the only U.S. state to commercially produce **olives**, with black olives being the most commonly grown variety. (Most of the olive oil consumed in the United States today is imported.)

- California harvested its first crop of **pistachios** in 1976, and never looked back. The nut is best adapted to the hot, drier regions of California and the Southwest, although California remains the major pistachio-producing state. (Iran dominates the market.)

- Due to its needs for special growing conditions, California is the only state that grows **pomegranates**. Only 5 percent of Americans have ever tasted one!

• The term *prune* refers to a whole dried plum. While plums can be grown outside California, the state produces nearly 100 percent of U.S. output of both table fruit and dried plums (i.e., **prunes**). This accounts for approximately 70 percent of world prune production.

• Like prunes, **raisins** are dried grapes. In the U.S., raisins are produced almost exclusively in the Fresno area. The United States has become the world's largest producer of raisins (although it trails Turkey and Iran as an exporter).

• California accounts for 99 percent of the **English walnuts** grown commercially in the U.S.

California Pepper Cups

Raw bell peppers make great serving containers! For this very green vegetable dip, use yellow, orange, or purple peppers for an eye-catching effect.

1 clove garlic, peeled
1-½ c. parsley sprigs
½ c. mayonnaise
3 tbsp. olive oil
3 tbsp. Parmesan cheese, grated
1 lg. bell pepper
vegetable "sticks" for dipping (peppers, carrots, celery, for example)

Combine garlic, parsley, mayonnaise, olive oil, and cheese in blender or food processor. Blend until smooth. Cut the top off the pepper; remove ribs and seeds carefully so as not to rip sides of pepper. Check to see if pepper will stand upright; if not, shave a little off the bottom. Fill pepper with dip mixture and serve with vegetable sticks.

A FEAST OF FESTIVALS!

JANUARY

MENDOCINO CRAB WINE DAYS (525 S. Main St., Ste. E, Ukiah 95482 / (707) 462-7417)

This ten-day event offers cooking classes from local chefs (plus crab specials in local restaurants), winery tours and tastings (plus pairing dinners), crabbing trips (meet local fishermen), whale watching, and lots more.

ZINFANDEL FESTIVAL (P.O. Box 1487, Rough & Ready 95975 / (530) 274-4900)

This four-day event celebrates what zinfandel producers call "California's State Wine" in an internationally recognized series of tastings involving 300 wineries. Even with space for over 10,000 attendees, the event usually sells out, so get tickets early.

FEBRUARY

HOLTVILLE CARROT FESTIVAL (101 W. Fifth St., Holtville 92250 / (760) 356-2923)

Holtville claims to be the carrot capital of the world, and to celebrate, it hosts a ten-day festival complete with golf tournament, Carrot Queen, carrot cook-off, arts and crafts, 5K run, live entertainment...even a parade! Besides, what else is there to do in February?

RIVERSIDE COUNTY FAIR AND NATIONAL DATE FESTIVAL (46-350 Arabia St., Indio 92201 / (800) 811-3247)

With everything a county fair has to offer (think magnificent rides) but with a twist: it's all done as an Arabian Nights theme. You'll love the camel races and don't miss the crowning of Queen Sheherazade. There's also cooking with dates and educational exhibits, plus long-time tradition the Blessing of the Dates ceremony.

SAN FRANCISCO CRABFEST (900 Market St., San Francisco 94102 / (415) 391-2000)

Held in venues all over the Bay Area throughout the month of February. With local neighborhood events, world-renowned participating restaurants, and starring the crustaceans themselves, February is the right month to be in San Francisco! (Wrong month to be a crab...)

SANTA CRUZ CLAM CHOWDER COOK OFF AND FESTIVAL (400 Beach St., Santa Cruz 95060 / (831) 423-5590)

Held at the world-famous Santa Cruz Boardwalk, competitors come from all over the state to participate, while attendees get to enjoy the fruits of their labors.

MARCH

WORLD OF PINOT NOIR (P.O. Box 1346, Arroyo Grande 93421 / (805) 489-1758)

Regular folks get to enjoy an environment usually reserved for members of the wine trade in this two-day event that includes panel discussions, tastings, pairings, and encounters with writers, winemakers, and passionate collectors.

APRIL

FALLBROOK AVOCADO FESTIVAL (233 E. Mission, Fallbrook 92028 / (760) 728-5845)
For over forty years, the folks in Fallbrook have celebrated the avocado in a popular one-day street fair with guacamole recipe competition, arts and crafts, food fair, and lots more. Held in April to coincide with the peak harvest.

BIG RED WEEKEND (P.O. Box 1601, Temecula 92593 / (951) 699-6586)
Purchase tickets for this special weekend wine-tasting event, the only one sponsored by a regional association that exclusively concentrates on red wines produced by its members. Visit more than twenty wineries and enjoy specially prepared dinners—and wine. Discount tickets for designated drivers.

O'REILLY'S OYSTER AND BEER FESTIVAL (1233 Polk St., San Francisco 94109 / (415) 928-1233)
The largest Celtic festival on the West Coast centers around the unique combination of oysters and stout, and offers hundreds of ways to enjoy both, as well as live music, Irish dancing, the suck and shuck competition, stilters, and cooking demonstrations. Special children's area too.

STOCKTON ASPARAGUS FESTIVAL   (311 E. Main St., Ste. 204, Stockton 95202 / (209) 644-3740)
Three days of live entertainment, arts and crafts, food and drink, golf tournament, cooking contests, and all kinds of spear-themed activities in this popular paean to the asparagus.

MAY

CASTROVILLE ARTICHOKE FESTIVAL (P.O. Box 1041, Castroville 95012 / (831) 633-2465)
Starting with a parade honoring the Artichoke Queen, this long-running (forty-seven years) festival includes a classic car show, farmer's market, cooking demonstrations and artichoke cook-off, arts and crafts, wine tasting, musical entertainment, children's activities, and much, much more.

CALIFORNIA STRAWBERRY FESTIVAL (1661 Pacific Ave. #15, Oxnard 93033 / (805) 385-4739)
With strawberries—and luscious recipes featuring the berry—in the starring role, this festival is one of the most popular in California. Contests, live entertainment, Strawberryland for kids, and more.

When you have a Dungeness crab at one of the many crab stands at Fisherman's Wharf, you'll enjoy a San Francisco experience that has changed little over the past 100 years. A freshly caught crab is dropped into a pot of boiling water, and when the shell changes from yellow to red, it's ready to eat on the spot!

JUNE

CHINESE FOOD FESTIVAL (727 N. BROADWAY, STE. 208, LOS ANGELES 90012 / (213) 680-0243)
Taste the very best authentic Chinese food and enjoy the many charms of Los Angeles Chinatown in this two-day event.

MONTEREY WINE FESTIVAL (2 PORTOLA PLAZA, MONTEREY 93940 / (831) 649-6544)
Billing itself as America's Original Wine Festival, this longtime event for professionals and buffs alike celebrates world-class California wine with educational seminars, cooking demonstrations by notable chefs, a live wine auction, and, of course, exquisite dining. Includes more than 120 California wineries pouring more than 800 wines.

OJAI WINE FESTIVAL (P.O. BOX 1501, OJAI 93024 / (800) 648-4881)
For over twenty years they've been celebrating the fruit of the vine in tiny Ojai with this one-day fund-raising event featuring over forty wineries.

NORTH BEACH FESTIVAL (556 COLUMBUS AVE., SAN FRANCISCO 94133 / (415) 989-2220)
San Francisco's Little Italy has been celebrating pasta and more for over fifty years with live entertainment, arts and crafts, Italian street chalk art competition, poetry, celebrity pizza toss, celebrity chefs, and lots more.

JULY

CALIFORNIA PEACH FESTIVAL (P.O. BOX 3231, YUBA CITY 95992)
Over 35,000 people crowd into tiny, historic Marysville at the peak time for ripeness to enjoy live music, arts and crafts, 5K run, farmer's market, pancake breakfast—and peaches, peaches, peaches.

FESTIVAL OF ART AND WINE (P.O. BOX 1862, SEBASTOPOL 95473 / (707) 824-8717)
Held in a quaint old railroad town on the Russian River in the heart of California's wine country, this premier fine arts festival features local wineries and regional musicians too. A highlight of the show is the rubber duckie race!

GILROY GARLIC FESTIVAL (7473 MONTEREY ST., GILROY 95020 / (408) 842-1625)
Feast on food laced with fresh garlic at this twenty-five-year-old festival where you'll also enjoy live music on three stages, arts and crafts, the great garlic cook-off, celebrity cooking demonstrations—and the Miss Gilroy Garlic pageant. Did we mention the garlic?

AUGUST

BODEGA SEAFOOD, ART, AND WINE FESTIVAL (P.O. Box 1862, Sebastopol 95473 / (707) 824-8717)
In the historic village where Hitchcock's The Birds was filmed, you'll find thousands converging to enjoy the best of the wineries, arts and crafts, and chefs in a rural outdoor setting with live music and more!

TOMATO FESTIVAL AND WEST COAST BARBEQUE CHAMPIONSHIP (1000 TEXAS ST., STE. D, FAIRFIELD 94533 / (707) 422-0103)
Features "Tomato Alley," where more than fifty varieties of heirloom tomatoes

and gourmet tomato products can be sampled and purchased, plus arts and crafts, live music on two stages, tomato cook-off, activities for kids. Special treat: all four Attack of the Killer Tomatoes *films are shown free all day!*

SEPTEMBER

ITALIAN FAMILY FESTA (425 N. FOURTH ST., SAN JOSE 95112 / (408) 293-7122)
Experience a little bit of Italy at this twenty-seven year old celebration featuring authentic Italian foods, continuous entertainment, arts and crafts, raffle prizes, grape-stomping contest, children's games, a tarantella contest, and great food.

OCTOBER

CALIFORNIA AVOCADO FESTIVAL (P.O. BOX 146, CARPINTERIA 93014-0146 / (805) 684-0038)
For over twenty years the Avocado Festival has been celebrating all things green with a golf tournament, cooking contest, arts and crafts, kids' activities, and live music all day long for three days; it's one of the largest festivals in California.

LOOSE GOOSE WINE FESTIVAL (23520 Bridgeport Ln., Santa Clarita 91355 (661) 799-9463)
Upscale wine festival in the Los Angeles area, with four days of wine pairing dinners, a golf tournament, live music, black-tie gala, and main event wine tasting. Make it a weekend and stay in charming Santa Clarita.

EASY GUACAMOLE

2 ripe avocados, peeled, seeded, mashed
½ c. finely chopped onion
2 tbsp. finely chopped fresh cilantro
1 tbsp. fresh lemon or lime juice
½ tsp. salt
½ tsp. garlic powder

Mix ingredients together and refrigerate until time to serve (be sure to put the plastic wrap directly on the surface to prevent oxidation).

For a spicier guac, add ¼ c. store-bought salsa!

NOVEMBER

WINE AND MUSHROOM FESTIVAL (525 S. MAIN ST., STE. E, UKIAH 95482 / (707) 462-7417)
Taste dozens of fabulous edible mushrooms, plus take a walk in the woods with local gatherers; enjoy local chefs' offerings, cooking classes, and learn wine pairing from vintners too. Special discounts with the Wine and Mushroom Passport!

CAL EXPO AND SACRAMENTO COOKS! (1600 EXPOSITION BLVD., SACRAMENTO 95815 / (916) 263-3000)
Culinary enthusiasts, gourmet chefs, foodies, and just about anyone interested in the kitchen will enjoy this one-day event featuring top-notch chefs and experts as well as the best and newest in food products, kitchen appliances, and implements. Bring your appetite too—there's lots of tasting to be done!

What's a Pomegranate?

You see them in the produce section at Christmas, and you've always wondered... besides looking great in a centerpiece arrangement, what the heck is a pomegranate, and what is it good for?

We're so glad you asked! Cultivated around the Mediterranean region for millennia, the pomegranate was brought to California by the Spanish missionaries in the 1700s. Today California is the only state in the union that produces the zesty fruit. Used extensively in Middle Eastern cuisine, the charms of the pomegranate are only now becoming known to Americans (aside from bartenders, who use grenadine syrup in some cocktails).

But listen to this: one pomegranate can supply 40 percent of your vitamin C requirement! It's a rich source of folic acid and is high in polyphenols (antioxidants). You may find commercially prepared pomegranate juice at your local grocery, as the health benefits become more widely known. So next time you see a beautiful red pomegranate, take one home—for your health!

NO FUSS, NO MUSS

Skinning a pomegranate is easy!

1. Cut off the crown, then cut pomegranate into sections.
2. Place a section in a bowl of water, then roll the dark red seed casings (called arils) out of the thin rind. Seeds will fall to the bottom while the paper-like rind will float.
3. Discard the rind, strain the water—eat the arils (seeds and all).
4. Yum!

Spicy Pomegranate Relish

1-½ c. pomegranate arils (seed casings) (about 2 pomegranates)

½ c. onion, finely chopped

1-½ tbsp. jalapeño pepper, finely chopped

1 tbsp. lemon juice

1 tbsp. sugar

¼ tsp. sea salt

Mix ingredients together gently. Serve as relish with meats or double the recipe and use as a salsa with corn chips.

Sunshine Salad

Those gelatin salads that mom used to make are just as popular as ever—especially on hot summer days. Here are two variations on the beloved Sunshine Salad!

Sunshine Veggie Salad 1

1-20 oz. can crushed pineapple
1 small pkg. lemon or orange gelatin
1 c. hot water
1 c. pineapple juice
½ c. grated raw carrots
½ c. finely chopped pecans

Drain the crushed pineapple and reserve the juice (add water to the juice if needed to make 1 cup). Dissolve the gelatin in hot water. Add the pineapple juice or the pineapple juice/water mixture; chill until slightly thickened. Stir in the grated carrots, pineapple, and nuts. Return to refrigerator and chill until firm.

Sunshine Dessert Salad 2

1 lb. small curd cottage cheese
8 oz. can crushed pineapple, well drained
1 c. mandarin orange sections
⅔ c. chopped pecans
½ c. grated coconut
9 oz. frozen whipped topping, thawed
3 oz. pkg. orange gelatin (dry)

Blend together cottage cheese, pineapple, oranges, pecans, coconut, and whipped topping. Sprinkle gelatin over this mixture and fold in well. Spread mixture in an 8 x 8 inch glass pan and refrigerate overnight. Serve on romaine lettuce leaves.

ARMENIAN DIASPORA IS GOOD FOR CALIFORNIA

After suffering waves of ethnic cleansing in the late nineteenth and early twentieth century, tens of thousands of Armenians immigrated to other nations—including the U.S. California is home to roughly half the one million Diaspora Armenians who have settled here, with large concentrations in Fresno, Glendale, Los Angeles, and San Francisco.

Lucky for us! Armenian farmers played key roles in developing the fig industry in the state, as well as grapes, raisins, and bulgur wheat—crops that had thrived in their homeland. Check out these delicious Armenian recipes!

ARMENIANS YOU MIGHT KNOW!

Cher (El Centro), singer, actress

George Deukmejian (Long Beach), former governor

Kirk Kerkorian (Fresno), billionaire

William Saroyan (Fresno), author

Apple Dolma

Serve with ham, pork, or turkey.

10–15 apples, depending on size
1 c. granulated sugar
4 c. water
1 tsp. kosher salt
2 c. water, boiling

½ c. rice
½ c. raisins
¼ tsp. cinnamon
¼ c. butter, melted

Preheat oven to 350°. Cut off tops of apples and reserve, then core apples, leaving reservoir 1 to 1-½ inch in diameter. Sprinkle one-quarter of the sugar into the holes. Meanwhile, bring water to boil over high heat; add salt and rice to fully boiling water and cover. Cook for 10 minutes. Add raisins and cook for 5 min. more, then remove from heat and drain extra water. Add ¼ cup sugar, cinnamon, and butter to rice mixture, stir to mix. Fill apples with rice mixture and add a pinch of cinnamon to the top of each. Replace the apple tops and arrange in a baking dish. Bring 2 cups water to boil and add remaining sugar; stir to dissolve, then remove from heat. Pour sugar water over apples.

Cover dish with foil and bake in oven approximately 30 min. Baste apples occasionally with liquid. Then remove cover and bake uncovered for approximately 10 minutes more.

Mahdzoon Chicken

Yogurt makes this chicken moist and tender!

1 c. olive oil

1 tsp. fresh garlic, crushed

½ c. dry white wine

1 tsp. fresh basil, chopped

2 lbs. boneless, skinless chicken breasts

2 medium yellow onions, thinly sliced

Salt and pepper to taste

2 c. mahdzoon (or plain yogurt)

½ c. Armenian or Italian flat leaf parsley, chopped

FORTY PERCENT OF GLENDALE'S 207,007 POPULATION IS OF ARMENIAN DESCENT—THE LARGEST NUMBER OF DIASPORA ARMENIANS ANYWHERE, AND THE SECOND LARGEST ARMENIAN COMMUNITY IN THE WORLD, AFTER YEREVAN

The night before, place oil, garlic, wine, and basil in a bowl; whisk together. Add chicken and turn to coat with marinade. Cover; marinate overnight in refrigerator. Heat skillet with 1 tbsp. of olive oil and brown the chicken on both sides. Discard rest of marinade. In separate pan, add 2 tbsp. olive oil and sauté onions until golden, adding salt and pepper to taste. Add browned chicken to onion, then spread yogurt over all. Cover and cook over medium heat for 30 minutes or until chicken is done. Sprinkle with chopped parsley and serve.

Honey, Let's Have Armenian Tonight

Here are two great restaurants smack dab in the center of California's largest Armenian populations—and they're always busy. Try them when you're in town!

Bedrosian Armenian Deli

3051 E. Ashlan Ave., Fresno 93726 / (559) 222-1626

Considered a local must-see, Johnnie Bedrosian's Deli is generally crowded with locals of Armenian extraction. The authentic dishes are superb and so is Johnnie—he's full of stories and loves to chat. Plan on staying for awhile!

Raffi's Place

211 E. Broadway St., Glendale 91205 / (818) 240-7411

With a reputation for the best kabobs in the Los Angeles area (and that's saying a lot!), Raffi's cozy little place is the most popular Armenian restaurant in Glendale. Dine inside or out, or get it to go, for lunch or dinner.

WHAT'S A CERTIFIED FARMERS MARKET?

It's simple, really: a CFM has been approved by the county agricultural commissioner and certifies that farmers offer for sale only those agricultural products they grow themselves. Some markets offer products trucked in from elsewhere, but a CFM market does not.

Meet Me at Third and Fairfax

Born in the dark years of the Depression, the Los Angeles Farmers Market was the brainchild of Roger Dahlhjelm and Fred Beck, two guys just trying to stay afloat during those cash-poor times. They envisioned a "village square" where local artisans and farmers could bring their products directly to an old-style market area ... problem was, they had no land and no money to build. But millionaire oilman E. B. Gilmore did, and in July of 1934 the first farmers—eighteen of them—pulled their battered trucks onto Gilmore's vacant lot at Third and Fairfax. There was no building—they displayed their produce on tailgates and old tables. Farmers were charged fifty cents a day to rent a spot. And the customers came.

The USDA estimates that average supermarket carrot travels 2,000 miles from field to table ... while most farmers market produce travels less than 50 miles to market!

Today the Farmers Market is a historic landmark, and "meet me at Third and Fairfax" is still a phrase heard on the lips of Los Angelenos. The clock tower built in 1941 is an icon, and the city has grown up around it. There is now an outdoor shopping mall, too. But most important, there are farmers, every day, selling homegrown produce to cooks and homemakers.

You're bound to see vegetables or fruits that you've never seen before at the farmers market—so ask the farmer about it! The market is a great place to get new ideas.

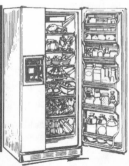

San Franciscso's Famous Chocolatier

Italian candymaker Domenico Ghirardelli had a bit of the wanderlust—leaving his native Italy at age 20, he traveled to Uruguay and then Peru before finding his way to San Francisco during the Gold Rush. In 1852 he established the Ghirardelli Chocolate Company in San Francisco—and it became an enormous success, partly due to Domenico's discovery that by hanging a bag of ground cacao beans in a warm room, the cocoa butter would easily separate from the chocolate. (This process, called the Broma process, is the industry standard today.) Today, Ghirardelli controls the entire manufacturing process, from cocoa beans to candy bar—one of the few chocolate companies in the country to do so.

Ghirardelli Square

Today it's one of San Francisco's best-loved landmarks, but in 1893, Ghirardelli Square was simply the location Domenico Ghirardelli's sons chose to expand the family company, purchasing an entire block of buildings. By the 1960s the company was purchased and moved—and before the block could be razed and turned into an apartment complex, two San Franciscans purchased the entire property. The historic brick structures were lovingly restored, and the block became a restaurant/retail complex that is considered to be the first "adaptive reuse" project in the country. In 1982, Ghirardelli Square became a National Historic Landmark.

You Won't Want to Miss This!

Every September, Ghirardelli Square hosts its Annual Ghirardelli Square Chocolate Festival, featuring chocolate delicacies from some of the best local restaurants and bakeries. Proceeds benefit Project Open Hand, which provides meals and groceries for those living with AIDS. Events include live music, children's activities, chef demonstrations—and all the chocolate you care to consume!

Squeezing the Melons...

Artichokes: A fresh artichoke will squeak when you rub a petal between your fingers.

Asparagus: Don't choose any that have dried, shriveled stems, particularly at the end.

Avocados: When it feels heavy, the oil content, which determines flavor, is high.

Beets: Best eaten right after picking; like corn, the sugar inside gradually turns to starch.

Blackberries: A ripe blackberry is shiny; the drupelets are large and plump.

Broccoli: The smell should mild and sweet, not strong; the cut end should not be dried out.

Cantaloupes: Beneath the raised pattern, the rind should be tan or gold, not green. Smelling helps too.

Eggplant: A shiny eggplant is fresh.

Green beans: If the pods stick to your clothes, they're fresh.

Hard-shelled squashes: A shiny rind means under-ripe squash; in the case of butternut, don't choose any with greenish streaks on the skin.

Parsnips: Parsnips should be stiff, firm, and white; if they've yellowed, they've been in storage.

Peas: Look for pods that are full but not to the point that you can see the shape of the peas inside.

Peaches: The background color should be golden yellow, with no hint of green.

Plums: When gently squeezed, they should bounce back.

Pomegranates: Cracks indicate that the fruit is so ripe it's about to burst.

Strawberries: Strawberries should be shiny.

Summer squash: If you can see a little juice coming out of the stem, the squash is really fresh.

Watermelon: Thump or slap it; it should sound like you've thumped a jug of water.

Walter Knott cultivated the world's first boysenberry, a combination of the red raspberry, blackberry, and loganberry.

In 1977 California had four farmers markets. Today there are over 400 certified farmers markets in the state, and more are being added every year!

Summer's a great time at the farmers market, but in California we often have year-round markets, thanks to our mild climate and long growing season. Don't ignore your farmers market when the days get short—they'll have lots of hard-to-find treats!

The number-one lost and found item at the farmers market is car keys! Make sure you know where yours are.

So What IS California Cuisine?

A lot of chefs have had a hand in shaping the restaurants that California has become famous for—and as a result there are a lot of definitions of California Cuisine.

Some say it's about letting the natural ingredients shine, without covering them in sauces or strong spices—let a zucchini be a zucchini, for example. Some say it's about freshness, which makes sense in a state that grows most of the nation's produce. Others say it's about health-consciousness: frying and battering are less prevalent in California cuisine (with the notable exception of tempura), or about presentation (it looks "too good to eat"!) And then some say it's about influences—California is where cuisine from Spain, Mexico, South America, and Asia and the Pacific Islands all meet with American palates, and those tastes invariably find their way into an inventive chef's repertoire.

We say it's a little of all that. California cuisine places an emphasis on using ingredients found locally, and using them while they're fresh. This means that menu items change frequently—often daily. It also takes different cooking styles and ingredients (particularly ingredients not commonly found else-

> Handling living food is so inspiring and energizing it makes you want to cook. You will never get tired of washing lettuce if it is beautiful to look at.
>
> —ALICE WATERS

where, such as fresh figs and dates, persimmons, or artichokes) and blends them in unexpected or nontraditional ways. Chef Alice Waters is generally credited with creating the California cuisine concept in her Berkeley restaurant, Chez Panisse. Wolfgang Puck made it popular by serving it to celebrities.

Chez Alice Waters

• Born in Chatham, New Jersey, in 1944, she graduated from UC–Berkeley with a degree in French Cultural Studies and later spent a year traveling in France.

• Alice opened Chez Panisse in 1971; the restaurant serves a single fixed-price menu that changes daily.

• Waters named her restaurant after a French movie character—from Marcel Pagnol's trilogy *Marius* (1931), *Fanny* (1932), and *Cesar* (1936)

• A strong proponent of farmers markets and sustainable agriculture, Waters has developed a network of regional farmers and producers who supply Chez Panisse and two other Waters restaurants: Chez Panisse Café (1980) and Café Fanny (1984).

• In 1996, Waters created the Chez Panisse Foundation to help underwrite cultural and educational programs, including the Edible Schoolyard program for children. It also funds the Garden Project at the San Francisco County Jail, which provide jobs for inmates and produce for the restaurants.

• Waters is the author (or coauthor) of several well-received books, including *Chez Panisse Cooking* (with Paul Bertolli) and *Chez Panisse Menu Cookbook*.

• Waters is also an International Governor of Slow Food; a visiting dean at the French Culinary Institute; an honorary trustee of the American Center for Food, Wine, and the Arts in Napa; board member of the San Francisco Ferry Plaza Farmers Market; and steering committee member of the Yale [University] Sustainable Food Project.

Menu

Chez Panisse

1517 Shattuck Ave., Berkeley 94709
(510) 548-5525

Monday – Saturday, for dinner.
Closed Sundays.

By reservation only,
as far ahead as one month;
a deposit is required.

Two seatings: 6:00 – 6:30 p.m.
and 8:30 – 9:30 p.m.

Menu changes daily.
Menu for the week is posted on Saturday.

A Place at the Table

Here are a few restaurants that specialize in California cuisine:

California Cuisine

1027 University Ave., San Diego 92103 / (619) 543-0790

This award-winning restaurant opened in 1982 and continues to serve up exactly what's promised by its name—fresh, inventive meals (there is neigher a freezer nor a can opener on the premises). The minimalist chic dining area allows the food to shine; if you want atmosphere, request the patio when you make your reservations.

Farmhouse Inn and Restaurant

7871 River Rd., Forestville 95436 / (707) 887-3300

Zagat's highest reviewed restaurant in a county teeming with exceptional dining experiences, the Farmhouse offers a California-French cuisine, artisan cheese, top-notch wine, and luxurious service.

The Fig Café

13690 Arnold Dr., Glen Ellen 95442 / (707) 938-2130

This sister to owner Sondra Bernstein's successful The Girl & The Fig offers affordable fine dining in a decidedly casual atmosphere. A popular and very unusual no-corkage-fee policy encourages diners to bring favorite wines from surrounding wineries.

Joe's

1023 Abbot Kinney Blvd., Venice 90291 / (310) 399-5811

For those who stay away from California gourmet for fear it's pricey, Joes's offers a four-course prix fixe meal that is both tasty and affordable—or try the brunch. Over 300 wines on the list make it easy to find a good accompaniment.

> **Opah** is Hawaiian for "moonfish." Native Hawaiians once believed that catching a moonfish was good luck; they would give it away as a symbol of goodwill.

Opah

26851 Aliso Creek Rd., Aliso Viejo, 92656-5315 / (949) 360-8822

This fresh and interesting seafood restaurant is a well-kept local secret that's long on all the important things—flavor, ambience, presentation—without a hint of pretension. Be sure to try the grilled opah, for which the restaurant is named.

Basic Lemon-Garlic Vinaigrette

3 cloves garlic
4 tbsp. lemon juice
3 tbsp. chopped fresh parsley
¾ c. olive oil
salt and pepper to taste

Smash garlic into paste with the flat edge of a knife. Combine garlic, lemon juice, and parsley, then whisk in oil. Season with salt and pepper. Use on salad of spring greens, for dipping artichokes, or as a light marinade for chicken or fish.

California in the Kitchen

Open-Faced Avocado Sandwiches

4 thick slices white artisan bread
1 ripe avocado, sliced
1 tomato, sliced
Fresh cilantro sprigs
Lemon-garlic vinaigrette or balsamic vinegar

On each slice of bread, layer sliced avocado and tomato. Drizzle lemon-garlic vinaigrette or balsamic vinegar over sandwiches. Top with a sprig of cilantro.

Note: avocado pairs nicely with bacon, and meat-lovers might enjoy the addition of two crisp slices as the first layer.

Did You Know...

Garlic is a member of the onion family.

Garlic crops are harvested and hung in sheds to dry before reaching their prime in early August.

Fresh garlic is hard to peel: as it dries it will shrivel inside the skin.

Studies have shown that garlic can suppress the growth of some tumors.

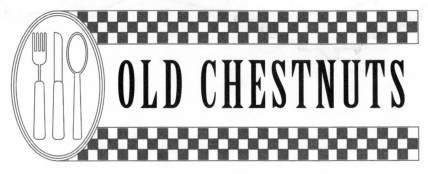

OLD CHESTNUTS

When the locals have been packing in for years, it's a very good sign! Here are a few "old chestnuts" we can recommend.

SAM'S GRILL / since 1867

374 BUSH ST., SAN FRANCISCO 94104 / (415) 421-0594

This San Francisco landmark serves up traditional seafood in a timeless, old-fashioned atmosphere.

Trivia: The Olympia Oyster Cocktail, a house specialty, isn't always available due to strict fishing limits—but if you dine on Mondays, when Sam's gets its shipment, you won't be disappointed.

BAY WOLF RESTAURANT / since 1975

3853 PIEDMONT AVE., OAKLAND 94611 / (510) 655-6004

For over thirty years this well-loved restaurant has been serving up a seasonal Mediterranean menu with extreme attention to every detail. Servers stay here for years, and know their business, so service is impeccable. Save room for dessert!

Trivia: Bay Wolf owners encourage all kitchen staff to read the books of Elizabeth David, a British cookery writer of the mid-twentieth century.

CASANOVA / since 1977

5TH ST. BETWEEN MISSION AND SAN CARLOS, CARMEL 93921 / (831) 625-0501

Intimate and romantic, with ambience to spare, Casanova features the cuisine of southern France and northern Italy in this acclaimed European-style restaurant owned and operated by a Belgian family. Every meal is unforgettable.

Trivia: Casanova was created in a tiny hundred-year-old home whose original inhabitant was once a cook for Charlie Chaplin. The wine cellar was hand dug under the remodeled house and now houses more than 30,000 bottles of wine!

MICHAEL'S / since 1979

1147 3RD ST., SANTA MONICA 90403 / (310) 451-0843

Chef-owner Michael McCarty is a pioneer of the California cuisine movement, and continues to serve up the freshest ingredients available in an unabashedly American menu with French and Italian influences. Ask to sit on the lush patio.

Trivia: Owner Michael McCarty was just twenty-five years old when he opened his restaurant on the beach in Santa Monica.

CAFÉ BIZOU / since 1994

14016 VENTURA BLVD., SHERMAN OAKS 91423 / (818) 788-3536

Elegant and very affordable, this French restaurant is beloved by locals and always crowded, so reservations are a must. For an astonishing bargain, add soup or salad to your entrée for just a dollar; wine corkage fee is an unheard-of two bucks.

Trivia: *Bizou* is French for "little kiss." Oo-la-la!

CHEZ MELANGE / since 1983

1716 S. PACIFIC COAST HWY., REDONDO BEACH 90277 / (310) 540-1222

This longtime local brasserie presents a casual, California-style menu made with high-quality ingredients, and is hailed as one of the South Bay's best restaurants. Located in the Palos Verde Inn.

Trivia: Learn how to make your favorite menu items next door at the Chez Melange School of Food and Wine.

DESIGNER PIZZA?

You heard us. But we don't mean that Donatella Versace got together in the kitchen with Ralph Lauren, although some pretty famous cooks pioneered the concept, starting with Alice Waters (of Chez Panisse). Waters installed a wood-burning pizza oven in her café in 1980, and began serving pizzas created with garden-fresh toppings. Eight hundred miles south in Los Angeles, Wolfgang Puck took that idea and ran with it, creating delicious pizzas with sometimes surprising ingredient combinations.

Also sometimes called California-style pizza (to distinguish it from, say, the thin-crusted New York–style, deep-dish Chicago-style, or even the square-cut St. Louis–style), designer pizzas are characterized not by the crust but by the use of nontraditional toppings like artichokes, barbeque chicken, or even peanut sauce. Adventurous chefs intrigued by a fusion of tastes have created Caribbean pizza topped with Jamaican jerk chicken, Thai pizza topped with bean sprouts and peanut sauce, or an alfredo pizza with a white creamy garlic sauce. (Puck's signature restaurant Spago in Beverly Hills has featured a pizza with smoked salmon and salmon caviar, and to this day pizzetta with spring onions and sorrel is a popular item at Chez Panisse.)

Now popularized nationwide (or at least in twenty-seven states, last time we checked) by the wildly successful California Pizza Kitchen, the designer pizza phenomenon is here to stay.

A TRUE CALIFORNIA PIZZA!

1 commercially prepared pizza crust (12 inches)
8 oz. mozzarella cheese, shredded
8 slices bacon, cooked, drained, and crumbled
½ lb. cooked chicken, shredded
2 ripe medium tomatoes, thinly sliced
1 avocado, peeled, seeded, thinly sliced

Preheat oven to 450 degrees F. Place large baking sheet on rack to heat for 30 minutes. Spread half of cheese on crust, then arrange bacon, chicken, and tomatoes on crust. Sprinkle remaining cheese over all. Transfer pizza to hot baking sheet, replace in oven and bake about 14 minutes, until bottom of crust is crisp and cheese on top melts. Remove from oven and arrange avocado on top of hot pizza. Allow pizza to cool for 5 minutes before slicing. Mama mia!

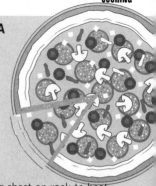

CALIFORNIA-STYLE BARBECUE CHICKEN PIZZA

1 commercially prepared pizza crust (12 inches)
2 tbsp. olive oil
2 large boneless chicken breast halves (approx. 1/2 lb.)
salt and pepper to taste
½ c. barbecue sauce (hickory-flavored is best)
7 oz. smoked Gouda cheese, shredded
¾ c. thinly sliced red onion
1 green pepper, thinly sliced

Preheat oven to 450 degrees F. Place large baking sheet on rack to heat for 30 minutes. Heat olive oil in heavy medium skillet over medium-high heat. Season chicken with salt and pepper, then sauté until just cooked through, about 5 minutes per side. Transfer chicken to plate; let rest 5 minutes, then cut crosswise into strips. Toss chicken strips with barbecue sauce. Spread half of cheese on crust, then arrange chicken on crust. Drizzle any remaining sauce over crust. Add onions and pepper, then sprinkle remaining cheese over all. Transfer pizza to hot baking sheet, replace in oven and bake about 14 minutes, until bottom of crust is crisp and cheese on top melts. Let pizza stand 5 minutes before slicing.

FROM THE COURTROOM TO THE KITCHEN

When former lawyers Larry Flax and Rick Rosenfield opened their first California Pizza Kitchen in Beverly Hills in 1985, they knew they were doing something different ... but they had no idea they would be bringing California-style pizza to the nation. But thank heaven they did!

That first restaurant—a bright, cheerful setting dominated by an open, wood-burning kitchen—was a runaway success, and new locations in the Los Angeles area soon followed. The point, they say, was not so much a pizza with such wildly inventive ingredients that diners couldn't imagine what the pizza would taste like. Celebrity chefs have that market cornered. Instead, they create combinations that diners can easily imagine and mentally taste—like their "Original BBQ Chicken Pizza" that also features sliced red onion, cilantro, and smoked gouda cheese, or "Thai Chicken Pizza" (with chicken marinated in a peanut sauce, bean sprouts, and roast peanuts). Want a traditional Neapolitan pizza pie? CPK has those, too.

Sound good? CPK has 188 locations, seventy-two of them in California alone (and that doesn't count California Pizza Kitchen ASAP locations, smaller restaurants in high-traffic areas like airports that serve from a smaller a menu of popular items).

BORN iN CaLiFORNia!

These popular restaurant chains all got their start in the Golden State. Some have expanded nationwide, while a few are the envy of non-Californians ...

A&W / FOUNDED 1922, LODI

Roy Allen started brewing his famous root beer in 1919, and selling it at his roadside stand. When he took on partner Frank Wright to open a restaurant on the site, a name and a concept was born. By 1960 there were 2,000 restaurants, mostly in Western states; at present there are over 600 A&W outlets in thirteen countries.

BIG BOY / FOUNDED 1936, GLENDALE

The first restaurant was Bob's Big Boy, named after founder Bob Wian. It's best known for its icon—a chubby boy in in red and white checked overalls, holding a double-decker hamburger.

CARL'S JR. / FOUNDED 1941, ANAHEIM

Founder Carl N. Karcher owned several hot dog stands in the Los Angeles area before he opened his first restaurant. By '56 he'd opened two Carl's Jr. restaurants, smaller versions of his restaurant. Currently there are more than 1,000 locations in thirteen states, Mexico, and Singapore.

DEL TACO / FOUNDED 1964, BARSTOW

Ed Hackbarth has three sons whose first names begin with D, E, and L, which is how Ed named his first taco restaurant. A few months later, he added a second restaurant; Now there are 179 franchised and 262 company-owned restaurants.

DENNY'S / FOUNDED 1953, LAKEWOOD

Although this chain started business as Danny's Donuts, founder Harold Butler had twenty restaurants by 1959, when he renamed the chain Denny's. Now, Denny's Corporation operates 2,500 restaurants worldwide.

FATBURGER / FOUNDED 1952, LOS ANGELES

Billing itself as the last great hamburger stand, Fatburger still cooks burgers one at a time, the way founder Lovie Yancey did at her first Los Angeles location. Franchise operations began in 1980, and over eighty-plus restaurants.

IN-N-OUT BURGER / FOUNDED 1948, BALDWIN PARK

Still a family-owned company, the first In-N-Out Burger was opened by Harry and Esther Snyder and featured a two-way speaker box for ordering, in an era when carhops were the norm. With 200 stores open, there are still no plans to franchise.

IHOP / founded 1958, Toluca Lake
First called International House of Pancakes, these Southern California restaurants featured German (lemon butter), French (orange sauce) and Swedish (with ligonberries) pancake breakfasts, among others. With the name now shortened to IHOP, the company presides over 1,252 IHOP restaurants in forty-eight states and Canada (most franchised), and is based in Glendale.

JACK IN THE BOX / FOUNDED 1951, SAN DIEGO
Founded by Robert O. Peterson, this tiny restaurant took orders from passersby through an intercom, selling 18-cent hamburgers. Now the company has 2,062 locations in seventeen states.

Follow the trail of the palm trees...

MARIE CALLENDER'S / FOUNDED 1947, LONG BEACH
Beginning as a wholesaler of pies made by mom Marie, founder Don Callender eventually opened a retail pie outlet and then a pie-and-coffee shop in 1964. Now there are 139 full-service restaurants nationwide.

McDONALD'S / FOUNDED 1940, SAN BERNARDINO
Brothers Dick and Mac McDonald had a hot dog stand first, but they hit their stride with their first hamburger restaurant. Beginning franchise operations in 1953 with Ray Kroc in charge, they were later bought out by Kroc.

ORIGINAL TOMMY'S / FOUNDED 1946, LOS ANGELES
The son of Greek immigrants, Tom Koulax served burgers and fries smothered in chili at his first hamburger stand—which is still standing!

TACO BELL / FOUNDED 1962, DOWNEY
Founder Glen Bell had been in the business for fifteen years, selling hot dogs and later tacos, before opening the first Taco Bell.

WIENERSCHNITZEL / FOUNDED 1961, WILMINGTON
Founder John Galardi's original hot dog stand on the Pacific Coast Highway is still in operation.

A Wienerschnitzel located in Sunnyvale, CA.

WINCHELL'S / FOUNDED 1948, TEMPLE CITY
Founded by Verne Winchell, who later went on to helm Denny's Restaurants, this popular donut operation started in a tiny L.A. County town.

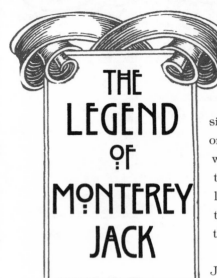

THE LEGEND OF MONTEREY JACK

Monterey Jack is the definitive Californian cheese, a variation of a cheese produced in the California missions 200 years ago. Called *queso del pais*, or "country cheese," this soft, mild cheese was well-known up and down the mission trail. After the Spanish missionaries left, local farmers and householders continued this method of cheesemaking, and during the 1800s its popularity spread.

Meanwhile, Scottish immigrant David Jacks had arrived in California in 1849, and by the 1880s was a successful land baron. Called colorful or notorious—depending on whether you liked him or not—Jacks had built up a large estate in Monterey, and in 1882 began shipping cheese from his estate in Monterey to San Francisco and other western markets. Each cheese was branded with the city of origin and Jacks's last name, and soon enough, folks were asking for "Monterey Jack" (the "s" got dropped).

Today, more than a third of California's cheesemakers produce some variation of Jack cheese although, ironically, Monterey Jack is no longer made in Monterey!

Warm Cali-Mex Dip

1 medium onion, chopped fine
2 tbsp. butter
1 large can diced tomatoes, undrained
1 small can peeled chopped green chiles
salt and pepper to taste
½ lb. Monterey Jack cheese, cubed
1 c. light cream

Lightly sauté and wilt onion in butter over medium heat. Add tomatoes, chiles, salt and pepper; simmer for 15 minutes, then add cubed cheese. When cheese just begins to melt, add cream and stir lightly, then turn into serving bowl. Serve with thick yellow corn chips. Recipe can be easily doubled. For neatness, serve in small individual bowls!

WHO CUT THE CHEESE?

CALIFORNIA ...

- is the nation's leading milk-producing state and in 2005 produced 37.5 billion pounds. (Take that, Wisconsin!)
- is the second-largest cheese-producing state in the U.S.
- produces 23 percent of the cheese produced in the U.S.
- is home to more than 50 cheesemakers who produce 250 varieties and styles of cheese.
- cheesemakers produce more Monterey Jack than any other state (in 2005, 332 million pounds).
- produces 17 percent of the cheddar made in the U.S.
- produced 2.14 billion pounds of cheese in 2005.
- is the largest producer of Hispanic-style cheeses, producing 96.3 million pounds of it in more than 25 varieties and styles.
- is the country's leading producer of mozzarella, producing 32 percent of the U.S. total in 2005.

AND...

- Forty-eight percent of all California cow's milk goes to make cheese.
- California cheese production in 2005 was: 45 percent mozzarella, 24 percent cheddar, 16 percent Monterey Jack, 5 percent Hispanic, 3 percent Parmesan, 2 percent provolone, and 5 percent other types.
- In 2005, U.S. per capita cheese consumption was 31.4 pounds, an increase of more than four pounds per person in the past decade.

Sources: California Department of Food and Agriculture, USDA, and the California Milk Advisory Board

California-Style Fondue

1 medium clove garlic, peeled
1 lb. Swiss cheese, shredded
1 lb. Gruyere cheese, shredded
3 tbsp. all-purpose flour
2 tbsp. butter
2 c. dry white California wine
3 tbsp. kirsch or brandy (optional)
dash hot pepper sauce
1 large loaf French or other crusty bread, cut into pieces (all pieces should have some crust)
Assorted fresh, raw California vegetables, cut into pieces*

Rub a fondue pot with garlic clove, then crush remaining garlic and set aside. In medium-sized bowl, toss cheeses with flour and set aside. Put butter and crushed garlic into fondue pot and cook over low heat about 10 minutes; add wine and raise heat to medium. When wine begins to bubble, begin adding shredded cheeses. Stir constantly until all cheese is melted. Add kirsch or brandy, if desired, and hot pepper sauce; cook 10 minutes more, until heated through. Place pot over low heat source for serving. Serve with fondue forks for guests to use to dip bread and vegetables into fondue.

* broccoli, carrots, cauliflower, peppers, sweet red onions, or your favorites!

Here's one that dates from the suburban San Joaquin Valley of the '60s—when Mom was a Valley Girl herself!

Valley Girl Cheese Ball

1 lb. Velveeta
3 oz. cream cheese
2 tbsp. finely chopped pecans
1 clove finely chopped garlic
Chili powder
Butter crackers for spreading

Mix cheeses, nuts, and pecans by squishing together by hand, then shape into smooth ball. Sprinkle all over with chili powder, then wrap in plastic wrap and place in refrigerator for 24 hours before serving. Spread on butter crackers (such as Ritz) for a yummy party snack!

YOU DON'T SAY!

- It's the third largest state (after Alaska and Texas), encompassing 158,302 square miles.

- At its widest point, California is 250 miles wide.

- About 35 percent of the state's total surface area is covered by forests.

- You'd have to travel 770 miles to go from the border of Mexico to the Oregon state line.

- California's highest point is Mount Whitney, in the Sierra Nevada range, at 14,505 feet. Actually, Mt. Whitney is the highest point in the contiguous United States!

- The lowest point in the state is just 76 miles away from the highest point (Mt. Whitney), and is at Badwater Basin, in Death Valley. It's 282 feet below sea level and is also the lowest point in the continental U.S.

- California borders the Pacific Ocean, Oregon, Nevada, Arizona, and the Mexican state of Baja California.

- The largest lake by area is Clear Lake, while the largest lake by volume is Lake Tahoe.

- The most southerly glacier in the United States is Palisade Glacier, located in California's Sierra Nevadas.

- The geographic center of the state is a point near North Fork.

California's 12 Geographic Provinces

Northern California
- Klamath Mountains
- Cascade Range
- Modoc Plateau
- Basin and Range
- Coast Ranges
- Central Valley
- Sierra Nevada

Southern California
- Transverse Ranges
- Los Angeles Basin
- Mojave Desert
- Peninsular Ranges
- Colorado Desert
- Channel Islands

Did You Know?

- California has a large salt lake, 376 square surface miles, called the Salton Sea. It's located in the Colorado Desert of Southern California.

- Sierra Nevada means "snowy range" in Spanish.

- The first ascent of Mount Whitney was in 1873, by John Muir.

CALIFORNIA'S NATURAL WONDERS

There are so many amazing natural wonders in California, we ended up arguing amongst ourselves about our favorites! Here are a few...

THE CHANNEL ISLANDS

This chain of eight islands off the coast of Southern California is a popular tourist destination and important wildlife refuge. Well, let's say that Catalina Island—the largest and only of the Channel Islands to be inhabited by man—is a popular tourist destination! In addition to the Channel Islands National Park, which is composed of San Miguel, Santa Rosa, Santa Cruz, Anacapa, and Santa Barbara islands, the area is one of the richest marine biospheres of the world, and the Channel Islands National Marine Sanctuary was established in 1980 to protect this amazing area. Several boating operators in the area offer cruises, island ferries to the park, charters, and whale watching expeditions too.

Interested in a resort experience instead? There are dozens of hotels, condos, and campgrounds on beautiful Catalina Island, and island activities include bicycling, boating, fishing, golf, hiking, kayaking, parasailing, sailing, SCUBA and snorkeling, tennis, and more, on your own or in tours. With a year-round Mediterranean climate, the Channel Islands are truly one of California's natural wonders.

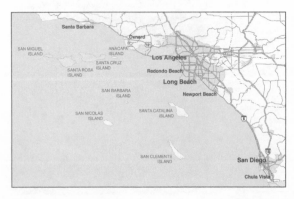

CALIFORNIA'S CHANNEL ISLANDS

Anacapa Island
San Clemente Island
San Miguel Island
San Nicolas Island
Santa Barbara Island
Santa Catalina Island
Santa Cruz Island
Santa Rosa Island

THE MOJAVE DESERT

Don't dismiss this magnificent site as "just" a desert, because it has a beauty all its own. For one thing, there are between 1,750 and 2,000 species of plants here—including the visually stunning Joshua tree—even though the desert gets less than six inches of rainfall per year. Spreading from California into Nevada and Utah, the Mojave Desert has two national parks (Joshua Tree and Death Valley); a wind turbine farm; several ghost towns (one is now a museum: Calico City); silver and borax mines; dry lakes that are vital wildlife habitats; two military installations; the historic town of Barstow on the old Route 66; and several alfalfa farming operations. It is, as well, the location of the lowest point in the forty-eight contiguous states: Badwater Basin in Death Valley.

Death Valley got its name in the winter of 1849, when a group of gold miners thought they'd take a shortcut on their way to Sacramento—but boy, were they wrong! They were lost for some weeks, and when one died, the name stuck. Due to prehistoric geographical activity, the valley is rich in minerals and contains some of the largest salt pans in the world. It's the nation's driest and hottest spot.

Racetrack Playa in the Mojave Desert.

The Mojave is also home to at least two mysteries: the singing sands at Kelso Dunes and the sailing stones at Racetrack Playa. The spectacular sand dunes at Kelso "sing" when visitors slide slowly down a dune; this generates a low-frequency rumble that can be both felt and heard as a low boom. Racetrack Playa (a *playa* is a seasonally dry lakebed) is so-named for the large rocks that move across its surface. Yep: rocks as big as a man move across the level surface of the playa. No one's ever seen it happen, no one's been able to photograph the actual movement despite years of interest, but the fact remains that the rocks move—at different times and for different distances.

Want to learn more? Visit the Mojave Desert for a look at Mother Nature in action!

YOSEMITE NATIONAL PARK

This beautiful park is internationally recognized for its gorgeous scenic views and abundance of hiking and rock climbing opportunities. It was the first wilderness area in America to receive national attention (and to be set aside by Abraham Lincoln in 1864) and was the focal point in the development of the concept of a national park service system. Yosemite became a national park on October 1, 1890. In 1984 it was designated a World Heritage Site.

It's difficult to describe in mere words the majesty of Yosemite, over 761,000 acres of largely unspoiled wilderness. Yosemite Valley, with the iconic El Capitan towering over it, is only one percent of the park, but it is where most visitors arrive and most stay. The valley has several hotels and historic lodges from which to explore the rest of the park. Old Half Dome, an impressive granite dome, is another famous image easily seen from the valley. But hike up into the high country, where you'll see Tuolumne and other meadows, crystal clear lakes, and spectacular waterfalls and mountain ranges. The park also has three groves of massive giant sequoia trees, some of the tallest and longest-lived trees in the world (coastal redwoods from the Northern California coast grow taller, and the Great Basin bristlecone pine of eastern California live longer—but who's counting?).

There are over 250 species of vertebrates living in the park's mixed coniferous forests—including the Sierra Nevada bighorn sheep living at high altitudes. So bring your hiking boots and a camera when you visit Yosemite National Park, one of the most beautiful places on earth.

Yosemite Valley, to me, is always a sunrise, a glitter of green and golden wonder in a vast edifice of stone and space.

—ANSEL ADAMS

YOSEMITE'S FAMOUS WATERFALLS

- Bridalveil Falls (620 feet)
- Chilnualna Falls (690 feet)
- Illilouette Fall (370 feet)
- Lehamite Falls (1,180 feet)
- Nevada Falls (594 feet)
- Ribbon Falls (1,612 feet)
- Royal Arch Cascade (1,250 feet)
- Sentinel Falls (1,920 feet)
- Silver Strand Falls (574 feet)
- Snow Creek Falls (2,140 feet)
- Staircase Falls (1,020 feet)
- Tueeulala Falls (840 feet)
- Vernal Falls (317 feet)
- Wapama Falls (1,700 feet)
- Waterwheel Falls (300 feet)
- Wildcat Falls (630 feet)
- Yosemite Falls (2,425 feet)

ANSEL ADAMS AND YOSEMITE

A committed environmentalist as well as a celebrated photographer, San Francisco native Ansel Adams (1902–1984) made Yosemite Valley accessible to everyone with his dramatic black-and-white photographs. He was an avid mountaineer and it was on a visit to Yosemite in 1927 that his life's work and his passion came together as he photographed Half Dome for the first time.

LAKE TAHOE

The name alone has so much cachet that an American car manufacturer named an SUV after it—but that won't ever be confused for the glory that is Lake Tahoe. Native Americans had lived on the banks of the lake for thousands of years, of course, but it was "discovered" by Kit Carson and John C. Frémont in 1844. Tahoe is the second deepest—at 1,645 feet—lake in the U.S. (only Oregon's Crater Lake is deeper), and one of the highest, with an elevation of 6,229 feet. The lake is divided in the middle with the state of Nevada; two-thirds of it lies in California.

The public appreciated Lake Tahoe (then sometimes referred to as Lake Bigler) from the start, and with the discovery of silver in the area, a resort town (Tahoe City) was established in 1864. That was only the beginning. By the turn of the century, hotels were well established, and gambling casinos (on the Nevada side only!) added in the 1950s attracted even more tourists. Today, tourism is the primary industry, with beach and water activities in the summer and world-class skiing all winter long. Hiking and mountain biking are also popular activities in this magnificent location; one famous hiking trail is the Tahoe Rim Trail, a 165-mile path that circumnavigates the lake.

Tahoe's Major Ski Areas

- Alpine Meadows (CA)
- Boreal Ski Resort (CA)
- Diamond Peak (NV)
- Donner Ski Ranch (CA)
- Heavenly Mountain Resort (CA, NV)
- Homewood Ski Resort (CA)
- Kirkwood Ski Resort (CA)
- Mount Rose (NV)
- Northstar-at-Tahoe (CA)
- Sierra-at-Tahoe (CA)
- Squaw Valley (CA)
- Sugar Bowl Ski Resort (CA)

Squaw Valley overlookiong Lake Tahoe. (Photo: David Liu.)

I DIDN'T KNOW THAT ALMANAC CALIFORNIA EDITION 2007

RED ROCK CANYON STATE PARK

At the northwest corner of the Mojave Desert, Red Rock Canyon is a visually stunning location with floral displays in spring, desert cliffs and canyons, buttes, and dramatic, colorful rock formations that, in past eras, served as landmarks for nomadic indigenous peoples and more recently to wagon trains of the nineteenth century. The park protects prehistoric petroglyphs and significant paleontology sites, as well as the remains of mining sites from the 1890s.

Two nature preserves are home to wildlife that includes roadrunners, hawks, lizards, mice, and squirrels. Other activities include hiking, horseback riding, and camping. Just be sure to dress appropriately: it's a desert, but temperatures can be extreme—blazing hot on a summer day but freezing cold at night.

The otherworldly look of the main canyon and its tributary canyons has often been a filming location for movies, television shows, even music videos. Red Rock Canyon has portrayed both the American West and outer space planetscapes! But it's the natural beauty that will make this small national park one of your favorite spots.

Red Rock in the Movies (and TV)

Over 100 movies and television series have been filmed here (not to mention music videos); here are just a few...

- Airwolf (1984)
- Andromeda Strain, The (1971)
- Barnaby Jones (1973)
- Battlestar Galactica (1978)
- Beneath the Planet of the Apes (1970)
- Bonanza (1959)
- Bounty Hunter, The (1954)
- Buck Rogers (1939)
- Car, The (1977)
- Have Gun, Will Travel (1957)
- High Chaparral, The (1967)
- Holes (2003)
- K-Pax (2001)
- Lassie (1954)
- Lost in Space (1965)
- Man From Cheyenne (1942)
- Outlaw, The (1943)
- Rawhide (1959)
- Ten Commandments (1956)
- Under a Texas Moon (1930)
- Wagon Train (1957)
- Westworld (1973)

CALIFORNIA VOLCANOES

Amboy Crater / Mojave Desert (extinct)

Anacapa Island / Channel Islands

Cinder Cone / Lassen Volcanic National Park

Coso Volcanic Field /
Coso Mountain Range

Lassen Peak / Lassen Volcanic
National Park

Long Valley Caldera / Inyo
National Forest

Mammoth Mountain / Inyo National Forest

Medicine Lake Volcano / Cascade Range

Mono-Inyo Craters / Inyo National Forest

Mount Shasta / Cascade Range

Pisgah Crater / Mojave Desert

Schonchin Butte / Cascade Range

TYPES OF VOLCANOES

Plug Dome
Slowly oozing lava builds up around the vent, forming a dome that often plugs the vent.

Shield
A wide, shallow volcano with a gentle slope formed by fast-moving viscous lava flow; picture a warrior's shield lying on the ground.

Cinder Cone
Fragments blown up from a volcanic vent fall to earth and pile up in the shape of a cone, leaving a bowl-shaped crater at the summit.

Strato
The opposite of a shield volcano, formed by slow-moving lava; stratos are steep and tall.

LASSEN VOLCANIC NATIONAL PARK

A visit to this very active volcanic area is a living lesson in geology—not to mention a photographer's paradise. Located in the Cascades Range—home to Washington State's Mount St. Helens—Lassen Volcanic National Park is one of the few areas in the world where all four types of volcano can be found; in fact, Lassen Peak is believed to be the largest plug dome volcano in the world. The park was incorporated in 1916 because of its significance as a living volcanic landscape, and offers a look at shield, cinder cone, and stratovolcanoes too. The original volcano, Mount Tehama, was violently active and then collapsed in on itself in prehistoric times; all that's left is a two-mile wide caldera, with plenty of geothermal areas still active.

There's over 150 miles of trails as well as a scenic highway that provides access to the many volcanic wonders in the area—including Sulphur Works and Little Hot Springs Valley (these hydrothermal spots are heavy on the sulphur, so they smell like rotten eggs!); Bumpas Hell, with hot springs, fumaroles, (steam vents), and mud pots (hot, muddy depressions); Devils Kitchen, where the hot springs are so acidic they've eaten pits and holes in the bedrock; Terminal Geyser (not a true geyser, but a very cold spring flowing over a fumarole); Boiling Springs Lake, with hot springs, mudpots, and fumaroles along its west shore (the lake itself is warm); and Cinder Cone and the Fantastic Lava Beds (a lava flow from an eruption in 1650). There are four shield volcanoes in the park, too: Mount Harkness, Red Mountain, Prospect Peak, and Raker Peak, each of which are now topped by cinder cones. Lassen Peak itself is a plug dome.

Be sure to bring your camera! Because so many minerals are expelled to the surface, the earth becomes stained (yellow from sulphur, reddish or pink from iron compounds, for example); the colorful scene is often called a painted dune or—if it's a mud pot area—paint pots. In addition to the majestic mountainous scenery, the painted dunes are a sight to behold.

THE ROCK

Imagine growing up on an 18.86-acre island. Then imagine growing up on a tiny island ... and sharing it with famous—but vicious—criminals such as Al Capone and Robert Stroud. Sixty families lived on Alcatraz Island during its time as a federal prison (1933–1963), and many children grew up there. Although the island is teeming with wildlife, in the rock pools along the shore, in the bird colonies on the rocks, and in the sea itself, life there was isolated, and often dull (families weren't even allowed to have dogs or cats).

Alcatraz Island

Discovered by the Spanish in 1775 (the name *Alcatraz* comes from the Spanish word for *pelican*), the island became a U.S. military installation in 1850, and later a military prison, which was acquired by the federal government in 1933 to establish a federal penitentiary. Alcatraz housed inmates who had of a history of escape attempts or violent behavior, and were always transferred to the island from some other prison. It was not a pleasant destination. The prison was finally closed in early 1963 because it had become so expensive to maintain.

Alcatraz lives in the popular imagination thanks to a few movies starring the prison, but today the only people on the island are the thousands of tourists who ride the ferry boats out to tour the abandoned prison and view the nineteenth-century military fortifications, as well as to enjoy a unique scenic view of San Francisco Bay. The Rock is also the home of the first—and oldest operating—lighthouse on the West Coast.

STARRING ALCATRAZ

Movies on or about Alcatraz Island—rent one today!

Birdman of Alcatraz, 1962

The Enforcer, 1976

Escape From Alcatraz, 1979

Murder in the First, 1995

The Rock, 1996

X-Men: The Last Stand, 2006

SURF CITY USA

With its mild climate, Huntington Beach (pop. 195,000) is full of folks who love being outdoors, and, thanks to local ordinances regarding land use, it has the largest ratio of park area to person of any city in the United States. Although the city is full of parks and greenways, though, you'll find everyone down at the beach! Boasting one of the longest piers in the world—and the longest on the West Coast—Huntington Beach is the original "Surf City," and hosts the world surfing championships every year. But that's not all— Huntington Beach is also a popular destination for kite surfing, and the spacious beaches are home to AVP Pro Beach Volleyball and Van's World Championship of Skateboarding too. This means that Huntington Beach is the quintessential California beach town, with a large portion of the local economy devoted to servicing the thousands who come to town to catch a wave ... or just catch some rays. Come on in, dude, the water's fine!

GREAT BEACHES FOR SURFING

- Ben Weston Beach, Catalina Island
- Black's Beach, La Jolla
- Bolsa Chica State Beach, Huntington Beach
- Cowell Beach, Santa Cruz
- El Porto, Manhattan Beach
- Huntington City Beach, Huntington Beach
- Huntington State Beach, Huntington Beach
- Imperial Beach, Imperial Beach
- Lunada Bay, Palos Verdes
- Maverick's Beach, Half Moon Bay
- Pacifica State Beach/Linda Mar Beach, Pacifica
- Pleasure Point, Santa Cruz
- Redondo Beach, Redondo Beach
- San Clemente Beach, San Clemente
- Seal Beach Pier, Seal Beach
- Shark Harbor, Catalina Island
- Steamer Lane, Santa Cruz
- Stingray Bay ('Ray Bay), Seal Beach
- Torrey Pines State Beach, La Jolla
- Ventura Point, Ventura

San Clemente, California, is the surfing media capital of the world—**Surfing** magazine, **The Surfer's Journal**, and **Longboard** magazine are all located here (**Surfer** magazine is in nearby San Juan Capistrano). It's also an excellent surfing destination, and many of surfing's biggest names (Shane Beschen, Matt Archbold, Christian Fletcher, Mike Parsons...to name just a few) were raised here or are longtime residents.

Another City By the Bay

The city of Half Moon Bay is as well-known for its local produce—and the Pumpkin Festival that draws tens of thousands each year—as it is for the bay it is named for. The mild climate makes for successful agriculture, and the area abounds in nurseries and farms (in addition to pumpkins, artichokes do very well here), with roadside stands on every corner selling local produce. But take a stroll into the historic downtown area—where you'll find art galleries, boutiques, bed-and-breakfasts, wineries, and more—and you'll find yourself at the beach, where you can enjoy whale watching, horseback riding on the beach, bird refuges, and two lighthouses. Not to mention the killer Maverick's Breaks, which is the site of an invitation-only big wave surfing contest every winter.

SURFERS AND SHARKS: NOT BFF!

Marine biologists have long been pointing out what surfers are starting to hear: from below (that is, a shark's-eye view) a paddling surfer bears a striking resemblance to a sea turtle, the shark's favorite meal. And a shark can see its prey up to 100 feet away. Yikes!

So what's a dedicated beach bum to do? Camouflage the surfboard, of course! We know that some species of sea creatures are poisonous to sharks (or the sharks just think they taste bad!). Now there are companies that make stickers and design surfboards that look like these fish! Why didn't we think of that?

San Diego's Hotel del Coronado is one of the oldest and largest all-wooden buildings in California—and one of the last surviving symbols of an era. A massive Victorian beach resort built in 1887–1888 as a premier resort for the wealthy, the Hotel del Coronado sits right on the beach facing the Pacific and offers Old World–style hospitality. It's the largest beach resort on the North American Pacific Coast and was designated a National Historic Landmark in 1977 ... and truly must be experienced in order to be appreciated. So save those nickels and dimes and indulge in a few days at the beach—just like your great-grandparents did!

MOTTO: BEST OF EVERYTHING

HOTEL DEL CORONADO

HEADQUARTERS FOR THE ARMY AND NAVY POLO, TENNIS,

OUTDOOR SPORTS EVERY DAY IN THE YEAR.

GOLF, BATHING, BOATING, AND FISHING

WRITE FOR LITERATURE

H. F. NORCROSS, GENERAL AGENT
334 S. SPRING STREET, LOS ANGELES, CALIFORNIA

MORGAN ROSS, MANAGER
CORONADO BEACH ... CALIFORNIA

An old advertisement for the Hotel Del Coronado.

The Haunting of a Hotel

...del Coronado. That's right. In 1892, a young woman, Kate Morgan, checked in to what's now room 3312, hoping to meet her estranged husband there a few days later. He never arrived, and soon she was found shot dead on the hotel's steps. And that's not the only haunted room—3502 is also the home of strange occurrences (lights switching on and off, curtains moving on closed windows, objects moving, murmuring voices, cold breezes, and ghostly sightings). It turns out that a hotel maid, who had befriended Kate, stayed in 3502 ... and after Kate's death, she was never seen again. Feeling adventurous? Ask for Kate Morgan's room when you check in!

Nature at a Glance...

California is home to the world's tallest (coast redwood), largest (giant sequoia), and oldest (bristlecone pine) trees.

The oldest living thing in the world, the bristlecone pine, resides in the White Mountains of Southern California. The oldest single tree is called "Methuselah," located in the Inyo National Forest, and is estimated (by core samples) to be more than 4,750 years old. The U.S. Forest Service does not mark Methuselah, to protect it from vandals.

Coast redwoods are old (they can live up to 2,000 years), but their claim to fame is their height: they have been known to reach heights close to 400 feet. The current tallest is "Stratosphere Giant" in the Humboldt Redwoods State Park, at 370 feet.

The giant sequoia is the world's largest tree in terms of total volume. The largest in the world is the "General Sherman," located in the Giant Forest of Sequoia National Park. It is 274 feet tall, and approximately 2,200 years old. General Sherman has branches that are more than six feet thick—at its base, it has a diameter of thirty-six feet.

There are nineteen World Heritage Sites in the U.S., two of which are in California: Redwood National and State Park on the Northern California coast, and Yosemite National Park in the Sierra Nevada.

The oldest lake in North America, Mono Lake, is located in California's Basin and Range area. This geographical area also contains the Owens Valley, the deepest valley in North America (more than 10,000 feet deep).

Of the 545 National Wildlife Refuges in the U.S., forty-two are in California, making it second only to North Dakota.

It is possible to surf in the Pacific Ocean and snow ski on a mountain during the same winter day in Southern California—but it does take some planning to avoid getting stuck in traffic!

The Cascades Ranges, stretching from British Columbia to Northern California, are part of the Pacific Ring of Fire, the ring of volcanoes around the Pacific Ocean. All known volcanic eruptions in the continental United States have been from Cascade volcanoes; the last to erupt in California was Lassen Peak, from 1914 to 1921.

The small town of Parkfield, California (pop. 900), is located directly on the San Andreas Fault and has a magnitude 6.0 earthquake about every twenty-two years—in 1857, 1881, 1901, 1922, 1934, and 1966. The 1993 earthquake was late: it struck in 2004.

California's largest lake, the Salton Sea, was formed in 1905 when the swollen Colorado River breached a temporary canal and flowed into the Salton Basin for almost two years.

One Man's Trash Is Another Man's Treasure

About a million tourists visit San Simeon every year—also known as Hearst Castle. But what most of them don't know is there's another "castle" just six miles down the coast, and it, too, is a California State Historical Landmark!

You can't miss it. It has a great view of the ocean from a ridge in Cambria—and all the locals call it Nitt Witt Ridge. Artist/recluse Art Beal, who bought the lot in 1928, built his home almost entirely of salvaged materials—from that more famous construction site up the road, from beachcombing, from the nearby forest ... and from his neighbors. He was, after all, Cambria's garbage collector. And yes, there are more than a few beer cans and hubcaps used in the construction of Art's masterpiece. But there are quite a lot of abalone shells, too, and other natural treasures.

Beal carved the foundations and terraces out of the hillside using only a pick and shovel, and it took him the better part of fifty years to build the house you see today. Age forced him to leave the house in 1989 and he died in 1992 at age 96—and sadly, Nitt Witt Ridge sat empty for ten long years.

Today a new family has moved in. Like Beal, they work on the house constantly (those years of neglect were hard on it)—but unlike Beal (who would stand on the roof and shake his fist at gawkers), the O'Malleys offer tours of this eccentric castle by the sea. Call ahead: tours are by reservation only!

881 Hillcrest Dr., Cambria 93428 / (805) 927-2690

AH NATURE

San Francisco Bay Flyway Festival

MARE ISLAND, VALLEJO 94590 / (707) 557-9816

One weekend a year celebrates the migration of shorebirds, waterfowl, and other wildlife through San Pablo Bay, the largest bay in the San Francisco Bay Estuary. Public access offered to areas of San Francisco Bay's north shore normally closed to the public, as well as tours, exhibits, even arts.

JANUARY

California Duck Days

P.O. BOX 943, DAVIS 95617 / (530) 757-3780

Field trips in the Yolo Basin wetlands, workshops, children's activities, art show, and exhibition hall with displays.

FEBRUARY

Redwood Coast Whale & Jazz Festival

P.O. BOX 244, GUALALA 95445 / (707) 884-1080

Cool jazz, wine and microbrews, and exceptional spots to view the whales as they migrate south.

MARCH

Heron Festival, Art Show, and Wildflower Brunch

CLEAR LAKE STATED PARK, KELSEYVILLE 95451 / (800) 525-3743

A little of this, a little of that...plus boat tours, birding walks, night hikes and stargazing, featured speakers, jazz in the park, native plants hike, events especially for families, and, oh yes—the herons.

APRIL

Yosemite Birding Festival

P.O. BOX 230, EL PORTAL 95318 / (209) 379-2321

Field trips, reception, speakers, artists, ranger walks, book signings ... and best of all, it's in Yosemite National Park.

MAY

Walk on the Wildside

1624 HOOD-FRANKLIN ROAD, ELK GROVE 95757 / (916) 875-9453

Live music, live raptors and bats, live animals of all kinds, live birds on tours, plus special activities just for kids ... and it's all free, in areas normally closed to the public

JUNE

Mono Basin Bird Chautauqua

P.O. Box 29, Lee Vining 93541 / (760) 647-6595

A chautauqua provides higher education opportunities through the combination of lectures, concerts, and public events ... in one of the most intensively studied natural areas in California—the internationally known salt lake called Mono.

JULY

California Reptile Festival

Kern Valley Nature Festivals, P.O. Box 833, Weldon, CA 93283 / (760) 378-2531

One of California's finest remaining riparian forests is the site of this one-day event to observe and learn about some of the most interesting, unusual, misunderstood, and rarely seen animals of California.

AUGUST

Kern Valley Hummingbird Festival

P.O. Box 833, Weldon 93283 / (760) 378-2531

See six species at a peak time for hummers in the beautiful Kern River Preserve.

SEPTEMBER

Wings of the Warners Festival

P.O. Box 1610, Alturas 96101 / (530) 233-5085

Held at Modoc National Wildlife Refuge—and in conjunction with the Alturas Balloonfest—there's bird-banding, workshops, crafts, and food.

OCTOBER

Welcome Back Monarchs Day

Natural Bridges State Beach, W. Cliff Dr., Santa Cruz 95060 / (831) 423-4609

Arts and crafts, live music, active games for kids, food ... and lots and lots of butterflies returning to their winter location.

NOVEMBER

Sandhill Crane Festival

Woodbridge Ecological Reserve, Lodi 95240 / (916) 683-1700

Celebrating the sandhill crane migration at Isenberg Crane Reserve; includes lectures and viewing tours.

Pasadena Birdfest

1750 North Altadena Drive, Pasadena CA 91107, (626)355-9412

Workshops, field trips, butterflies, and birding in the scenic San Gabriel Valley.

Wild beasts and birds are by right not the property merely of people who are alive today, but the property of unknown generations whose belongings we have no right to squander.

—President Theodore Roosevelt

THRILLS, CHILLS, and SPILLS

For pure excitement, there's nothing quite like whitewater rafting, and California has some excellent venues. River rapids are classified according to degree of danger, from 1 to 5, so it's easy to choose the right experience. Whether you're an experienced rafter with your own equipment, or just a weekend adventurer on a tour, buckle up that life vest, strap on that helmet, and let's get wet!

RATING THE RAPIDS

Class 1 – Beginner   Class 2 – Intermediate

Class 3 – Moderate   Class 4 – Difficult   Class 5 – Advanced

GREAT WHITEWATER RAFTING ADVENTURES

Class 1
- American River, South Fork: in Coloma Valley, "floats" encounter gentle rapids and calm pools on this part of the river

Class 2
- American River, South Fork: particularly during spring run-off, a challenging but not overwhelming experience

Class 3
- Kings River: near Fresno, exciting but suitable for beginners
- Upper Merced River: in the Sierras near Yosemite, a roller coaster ride
- Trinity River: features like "Hell Hole," "The Slot," and "Zig-Zag" are a clue what you're in for!
- American River: in the Sierra foothills, featuring "Satan's Cesspool" and "Trouble-maker"

Class 4
- American River, Middle Fork: look out for Tunnel Chute, with a 6-ft. drop and 90-ft. rock tunnel
- American River, North Fork: this sheer canyon offers a 7-ft. falls for starters
- Kaweah River: nonstop action from the moment you put in, just staying in the raft is an accomplishment
- Stanislaus River, North Fork: exciting and beautiful, a high elevation that drops rapidly
- Tuolumne River: steep, technical rapids with names like "Rock Garden" and "Nemesis"
- Upper Kern River: the "Widow Maker" is just one rapids to watch out for

Class 5
- California Salmon River: one of the most difficult in the state, with rapids that are steep, powerful, and long
- Cherry Creek, Upper Tuolumne: often considered the most difficult whitewater in the U.S.
- Upper North Yuba River: near Lake Tahoe, through tight, high drops and boulder gardens

A Good Walk—Unspoiled!

With some of the most spectacular scenery on planet
earth, California offers incredible hiking opportunities—
some to destinations that would not otherwise be
seen. Here are eight excellent hikes for serious hikers.
Be sure to reserve backcountry wilderness permits
where necessary and remember—leave no trace.

1. Pacific Coast Trail / 2,650 miles
Running from Mexico all the way to Canada, the
PCT passes through the Mojave Desert, the Sierra
Nevada and Mt. Whitney, Yosemite National Park,
Marble Mountain and the Russian Wilderness in Northern California, and
the volcanoes of the Cascades including Mt. Shasta. Pick it up anywhere
along the route for a few hours or days!

2. High Sierra Trail / 49 miles
This trail starts at Crescent Meadow in Sequoia National Park and crosses
the Sierra Nevada from west to east, passing through remote areas that few
ever see. Be sure to plan a relaxation stop at Kern Hot Springs; if you've got
time, junction with the John Muir Trail and end at Mt. Whitney.

3. Mount Whitney / 22 miles
Experienced hikers can reach the highest peak in the contiguous United
States without technical mountaineering skills—an elevation of 14,505 feet!
Best to prepare for the altitude, though, by camping at higher elevations
before attempting the summit.

4. Half Dome / 16 miles
This iconic granite dome is definitely a workout, but most folks manage it:
the last 400 feet of smooth granite are embedded with bars and chains with
which to pull yourself up the 45-degree angle.

5. Cloud's Rest / 14.4 miles
Make your way to the Sunrise Lakes Trailhead at Tenaya Lake in Yosemite
National Park and hike to picturesque Cloud's Rest, where you'll have a
stunning view of Half Dome.

6. Bald Mountain / 6.4 miles
Take the Bald Mountain trail in Sugarloaf Ridge Stated Park for an inspiring look at the Sonoma and Napa Valleys—then reward yourself with a stop
at your favorite winery.

7. Ewoldsen Trail, Big Sur / 4.5 miles
Start in the parking lot of the Julia Pfeiffer Burns State Park and hike up
through coastal redwoods along McWay Creek; the summit offers a
panoramic view of the Pacific Ocean and coastal ranges.

8. Mastodon Peak, Joshua Tree National Park / 3 miles
A moderate hike that starts at the Cottonwood Spring Oasis and takes you
through mining country, where you'll see a desert spring, a historic mine
and mill site, and a monzogranite mound. You can see the Salton Sea from
the peak.

X-RATED GARDENING

Xeriscape gardening—sometimes jokingly referred to as "zero-scape" gardening—has become part of the California gardener's vocabulary. Coined by the Denver Water Department in 1983, the term and concept of water conservation and using drought-tolerant plants has swept the country. Increasing controls on potable watering coupled with periods of serious drought have made believers out of thousands.

The seven principles are Xeriscaping are:

1) start with good design
2) improve the soil
3) limit lawn areas
4) choose low-water need plants
5) water efficiently
6) mulch
7) practice good maintenance

Xeriscape gardening is good for you and good for the environment. Surf the Internet for good Web sites.

WATER-WISE PLANTS FOR CALIFORNIA

- Achillea
- Agastache
- Alyssum
- Anthemis
- Coreopsis
- Dianthus
- Gallardia
- Hellanthus
- Lavandula
- Penstemon
- Ratibida
- Salvia
- Santolina

For the Best Performance in the Garden, the Winner is....

ANNUALS

Ageratum (*Ageratum houstonianum*)

Alyssum (*Lobularia maritma*)

California Poppy (*Eschscholzia californica*)

Cosmos (*Cosmos bipinnatus*)

Icelandic Poppy (*Papaver nudicaule*)

Nasturium (*Tropaeolum majus*)

Pansy (*Viola x wittrockiana*)

Phlox (*Phlox drummondii*)

Sweet Peas (*Lathyrus odoratus*)

Wood Violets (*Viola odorata*)

Sweat Pea

PERENNIALS

Blue Marguerite Daisy (*Felicia amelloides*)

Candytuft (*Iberis sempervirens*)

Canna Lily (*Canna x generalis*)

Clivia Lily (*Clivia miniata*)

Coreopsis (*Coreopsis grandiflora*)

Daylily (*Hemerocallis x hybrids*)

Delphinium (*Delphinium elatum*)

Foxglove (*Digitalis purpurea*)

Impatiens (*Impatiens walleriana*)

Ivy Geranium (*Pelargonium peltatum*)

Lily of the Nile (*Agapanthus africanus*)

Shasta Daisy (*Chrysanthemum x superbum*)

Transvaal Daisy (*Gerbera jamesonii*)

Wallflower (*Erysimum linifoium*)

Daylily

Foxglove

(Source: *Bruce and Sharon Asakawa's California Gardener's Guide*, Cool Springs Press, 2000)

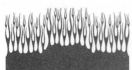 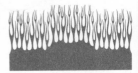

FIRE-FIGHTING PLANTS

In a state where wildfires are a real and always-present threat, priority number-one is to make your home as defensible as possible. This means creating a firebreak around your home, at least 30 feet wide, as well as keeping the area clear of litter (pine needles, underbrush, et cetera), trimming low-hanging branches over your roof—there are all kinds of tips. In fact, these "suggestions" might even be mandated by local laws—check it out.

While there is no such thing as a fireproof plant (anything will burn), these plants are fire-resistant and should be considered when you evaluate your landscape. Note that this list is not comprehensive; talk with your local nurseries, fire department, or the California Department of Forestry for more ideas.

Ground Covers
African Daisy – *Osteospermum fruticosum*
Creeping Rosemary – *Rosmarinus officinalis prostrata*
Dwarf Coyote Bush – *Baccharis pilularis prostratus*
Ice Plant – many kinds
Periwinkle – *Vinca minor; Vinca major*
Rock Rose – *Cistus vellosus*
Silver Mound – *Artemesis caucasica*
Snow in Summer – *Cerastium tomentosum*
Yarrow – *Achillea tomentosa*

Shrubs
Bearberry – *Arctostaphylos uva-ursi*
Carmel Creeper – *Ceanothus horizontalis*
Lemonade Berry – *Rhus integrifolia*
Oleander – *Nerium oleander*
Star Jasmine – *Trachelospermum* spp.

Trees
Brazilian Pepper – *Schinus terebinthifolia*
California Pepper – *Schinus molle*
Carob – *Ceratonia siliqua*

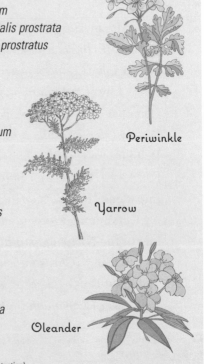

Periwinkle

Yarrow

Oleander

(Source: adapted from Calif. Dept. of Forestry and Fire Protection)

What's In a Name?

You don't have to be a Latin scholar to be a great gardener, but understanding the basics of the plant naming system is informative and it can really be fun! Every plant has a name—usually Latin—that identifies it and only it. The first part is the genus (think of it as the "generic" or family name). The second name is the species (or the "specific" name), which will identify the type of individual plant. Both are italic, initial upper case for the genus, and initial lower case for the species. (A possible third name may be a cultivar; it's enclosed within single quotes like this, *Acer rubrum* 'October Glory' and refers to a superior selection.) The really cool thing is that you'll quickly pick up clues as to what the plant is like. For example:

alba	= white
japonica	= originating in Japan
canadensis	= originating in Canada
citrinus	= lemon yellow color
lancifolia	= lance-shaped
crispula	= curled
undulata	= wavy
micro	= very small
serrata	= serrated leaves
variegata	= variegated
sempervirens	= evergreen
gracilis	= graceful

(Source: adapted from *Tennessee Gardener's Guide, Third Edition*, Judy Lowe, Cool Springs Press, 2001)

LATIN STUDIES
Horticulture
Definition: the science and art of growing fruits, vegetables, flowers, or ornamental plants. This word is also from the Latin: hortus (garden) and cultura (culture)!

The Top 20 Reasons to Love California

(as if You Needed Any...)

1. Mountains...ocean. 'Nuff said.
2. Yosemite National Park. It can make grown men weep.
3. The ringing bells on the San Francisco cable cars. Riding them is pretty cool too.
4. Watching the sunset from a beach in Southern California. No worries.
5. Best cantaloupes. Ever. Eaten warm, fresh from the field.
6. Disneyland. We had it first, and it's still the best. The Magic Kingdom really is magic.
7. Those magnificent California condors, flying high. And surviving.
8. Big Sur. It's not just a place, it's a state of mind.
9. Passionate politics. Californians care. And they get out and sign petitions.
10. Wine. Napa Valley, Santa Barbara ... California's got it goin' on.
11. The boardwalk at Santa Cruz. Just wear your sunscreen, please. Yes, Mom.
12. Hollywood! After all, where would we be without E.T., Ace Ventura, and the Terminator? *Oll be bock.*
13. California cuisine. It's good for you.
14. Sunrise at Lake Tahoe. Crisp, cool, clear, consummate.
15. The Hotel del Coronado. Who paints all that gingerbread, anyway?
16. Redwood forests. A gentle reminder that there really is something bigger than us.
17. Whale watching. It's a whole other world out there, and sometimes, if we're lucky, we get a glimpse of it.
18. Anacapa Island Arch Rock.
19. The weather. What's not to love?
20. The Golden Gate Bridge. It's perfect.

I DIDN'T KNOW THAT ALMANAC CALIFORNIA EDITION 2007